Read What Amazon Buyers Are Saying About
ACLS Certification Exam Q&A With Explanations

• 5.0 out of 5 stars

By L. Mon March 2, 2016

Very easy to read and understand. Would definitely recommend to others.

• 5.0 out of 5 stars

By Crazy Mom on October 16, 2015

I highly recommend this for ACLS renewal review!!!! This is a great study guide for ACLS or renewal. I read all the practice questions the night before and received a 98% on the test. The analysis of each answer really helped me understand and retain everything. I have since shared it with co-workers when they are due to renew their ACLS.

• 5.0 out of 5 stars

By JetPowers on April 25, 2015

Focused toward passing the exam. Face it, even if we run codes these questions can be tricky – and try to keep up with the ever changing AHA guidelines. The pre-amble to test questions is well organized easy reading, useful and interesting. The test answers with explanations speak for themselves. It's a great pre-course study guide for passing the certification exam and focused for that purpose

• 5.0 out of 5 stars

By Mark on April 21, 2015

Easy to follow. An outstanding guide. Helped me pass the course, easy to follow!!!! Highly recommended!!

• 5.0 out of 5 stars

By VCRN on December 15, 2015

This is a comprehensive yet concise review book. I have to recertify every two years and found it a great refresher course of the details of practice that we are consistently tested on but may not stick in memory. I can also appreciate its value for the first time student. It gave me confidence to go into class confident I knew what I was doing and could convey that when tested. Highly recommend it!

Read What Amazon Buyers Are Saying About
ACLS Certification Exam Q&A With Explanations

• 5.0 out of 5 stars

By Karen McKinney on May 4, 2015

This book is excellent. There are many practice questions to get you prepared. Lots of practical and usable information and advice about the ACLS class and exam. I highly recommend this book. Get it! You and your patient will be glad you did.

• 5.0 out of 5 stars

By Mina Markazi on April 21, 2015

Excellent book.

• 5.0 out of 5 stars

By Dale C. Pickart on September 21, 2015

Very helpful!

• 5.0 out of 5 stars

By Amazon Customer on January 6, 2016

Would recommend for everyone taking ACLS. Excellent study guide.

• 5.0 out of 5 stars

By Jaws on November 20, 2015

Looks good. Bought to prep for exams.

• 5.0 out of 5 stars

By OneDiamondForever on February 16, 2016

Dead on!! A great review!!

• 5.0 out of 5 stars

By Donna Leonard on January 21, 2016

As advertised.

Updated & Expanded For 2017

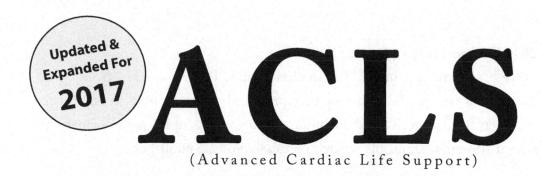

ACLS
(Advanced Cardiac Life Support)

CERTIFICATION EXAM
Q&A
WITH EXPLANATIONS

**FOR HEALTHCARE PROFESSIONALS AND STUDENTS
UPDATED USING THE LATEST GUIDELINES AND RESEARCH**

Michele G. Kunz, MSN, ANP, RN-BC
& Joseph C. Kunz, Jr., MBA
Foreword by Dr. Peter "Tucker" Woods, DO

Dickson Keanaghan, LLC
Long Island, New York

Publisher: Dickson Keanaghan, LLC, Long Island, New York
Website: EmpowermentEducation.com

Publication Date: November 01, 2016
Printed in the USA

College administrators and instructors, college bookstores, and book retailers, can order this book directly from Ingram.

Publisher's Cataloging-In-Publication Data

Names: Kunz, Michele G., author | Kunz, Joseph C. III., author. | Woods, Peter IV, foreword author.
Title: ACLS (Advanced Cardiac Life Support) certification exam Q&A with explanations : for healthcare professionals and students , updated using the latest guidelines and research / Michele G. Kunz, MSN, ANP, RN-BC; Joseph C. Kunz, Jr., MBA; foreword by Dr. Peter "Tucker" Woods, DO.
Description: "Updated and expanded for 2017." | Includes bibliographical references. | Long Island, NY: Dickson Keanaghan, LLC, 2016.
Identifiers: ISBN 978-1-933230-75-7 | LCCN 2016918240
Subjects: LCSH Advanced Cardiac Life Support --Examination, questions, etc. | Arrhythmias, Cardiac --Therapy -- Examination, questions, etc. | Cardiac arrest --Treatment--Examinations, questions, etc. | Cardiac resuscitation --Examinations, questions, etc. | Cardiac emergencies --Examinations, questions, etc. | BISAC MEDICAL / Emergency Medicine | MEDICAL / Education & Training | MEDICAL / Test Preparation & Review
Classification: LCC RC685.C173 .K86 2016 | DDC 616.1/2062 --dc23

Table Of Contents

Note: Dickson Keanaghan developed this book to be a living, evolving document, and as such, intends to update this document as needed, and as new content becomes available. We welcome your participation to keep this book up to date. If you know of more recent developments, or have suggestions for other topics to cover within this publication, please let us know. Contact JCKunzJr@DicksonKeanghan.com.

Foreword

"Charging... I am going to shock on three. One, I'm clear... Two, you're clear...Three, we're all clear." I will never forget the first time I had to utter those words during my first cardiac arrest.

There is nothing more intense - or intimidating for a newly trained provider - than delivering a jolt of electricity to a patient's body during resuscitation. Nonetheless, this action, and all the other actions of Advanced Cardiac Life Support (ACLS), can make the difference between life and death. That is the goal of ACLS - to save a life! But first, of course, you will need to pass the ACLS course and receive your certification.

This new book by Michele and Joseph Kunz will not only help ensure that you succeed in your ACLS certification, but more importantly it will help prepare you for real-life—your first "code." In fact, there is a section in the book entitled "10 Hot Tips for Surviving Your First Code."

In terms of learning and preparing for your ACLS exam, there is no "one size fits all" approach. Different people learn in different ways. Some learn by visual cues, some by watching videos, some by practicing question after question, some by using flash cards, etc. What impressed me most about this book is that there is something for everyone - regardless of your method of learning. Michele and Joe have provided a wide variety of useful tools that will allow you to become masters of the material. Included are more than 100 practice questions, YouTube videos, their famous *Zombie Notes Study Charts*, and numerous helpful tips.

While taking an ACLS examination can be daunting, this book will assist you from beginning to end by keeping things simple - removing the intimidation, the anxiety and the complexity. Michele and Joe have years of teaching experience in preparing students for these examinations, and their formula of keeping it simple and using straightforward approaches works.

As you read this book, you are bound to have "eureka moments" where you suddenly "get it" and are no longer confused about one or more ACLS processes that you had trouble understanding. The authors have a knack of explaining complex processes in an easy-to-understand method. Refreshing, too, are the ways in which they make it fun and functional, without any fluff. Michele goes so far as to make herself available at all times for email questions regarding the book, which demonstrates the extra mile the authors will go for ACLS students.

This book is absolutely perfect for someone who is taking the ACLS examination for the first time. It will become your "companion" during the entire examination-preparation process. At the same time, it is a great guide for those seeking re-certification. Even if you just want to refresh your ACLS knowledge you will find this book indispensable.

Ultimately, the Kunz's have created an essential book that is filled with practical and useful information. After reading it and applying their tips and techniques, you can feel confident during your examination that you will pass it on your first attempt. More importantly, you will be able to apply this knowledge and effectively treat life-threatening conditions outside of the classroom. Are we all clear?

Dr. Peter "Tucker" Woods, DO
CarePoint Health Emergency Department System Director
• Christ Hospital, Jersey City, NJ
• Hoboken University Medical Center, Hoboken, NJ
• Bayonne Medical Center, Bayonne, NJ

How This Book Will Help You Succeed

• This book will help you pass the ACLS certification exam on your first attempt.

• This book will help you build the strong foundation you need to begin to more fully understand and internalize the entire scope and importance of ACLS.

• We have created a video for every topic and article in this book, all available on YouTube.com/MicheleKunz.

• Lots of practical and usable information and advice about the ACLS class and exam.

• 101 practice questions that cover every possible medical and nursing scenario and topic on the ACLS certification exam.

• No confusing wrong answers to clutter your brain.

• Contains all the essential information for ACLS exam success.

• This book, together with Michele's YouTube videos, will greatly reduce your test-taking anxiety.

• All information in this book has been updated to the current guidelines.

• Michele is always available for your email questions about this book, or any aspect of nursing or hospital work.

• Hot tips for surviving your first code.

• Hot tips to help you memorize lots of new information.

• Learn all of the biggest myths about the AED.

Who This Book Is Meant For

All licensed healthcare providers and emergency responders such as:

• Physicians (MD's, DO's, DPM's)

• Nurses

• Paramedics

• Emergency Medical Technicians

• Physician's Assistants

• Procedural Technicians

• Nurse Practitioners

• Residents and Fellows

• Medical and Nursing Students

• Medical and Nursing Assistants

• Dentists

• For all licensed healthcare professionals

• Sleep Technicians

Introduction

Our newly revised and enhanced book for 2017 that you now hold in your hands, *ACLS Certification Exam Q&A With Explanations* will certainly help you pass any Advanced Life Support Certification Course. As you look through the book, you will quickly see that this book's format is different from all other review and test preparation books.

This book is specifically geared toward healthcare students and new healthcare professionals that are preparing to take the ACLS certification exam for the first time. This book will also give the seasoned healthcare professional lots of great review information as well as a way to update themselves on the latest research and guidelines.

Whichever certifying agency's program you are taking, either in a classroom or on the internet, this book will help you succeed in this course. In this book we give you all the essential information that you will need to successfully pass the certification course and exam on your first attempt.

Joe and I have been teaching this course to healthcare professionals and students since 1984. We know what works and what doesn't when it comes to helping our students be successful. Back then we had to develop almost all of the study materials for our students by ourselves because very little existed at the time. The *Zombie Notes Study Charts* were some of the first study aids we developed to help our students learn a large amount of information very quickly. We know that this format works very well because hundreds of thousands of healthcare professionals and students, in hospitals and colleges all over the world, have used this handy, no-nonsense chart to help them successfully pass the ACLS certification exam.

Therefore, in order for you to be successful on the certification exam, and on the job, we expect you to memorize every bit of information contained within the *Zombie Notes Study Charts* and within this book. It is essential that you know this information by heart and can recall it at a moment's notice. This information is not only essential for the exam, but for your career, and the survival of your patients, as well.

You will find that the key to passing the certification exam and course lies in applying your knowledge through questions and answers, not rote memory alone. Memorization is simply the first step to learning and committing the information to your long-term memory. You will find that studying our book, and our *Zombie Notes Study Charts*, and watching our YouTube videos, all combine to make a very powerful study system, and a very productive and quick way to prepare yourself for success on the exam.

Therefore, in this book, we have created 101 practice questions that are designed to simulate actual exam conditions. The subject of ACLS covers a lot of material. It is an interesting topic, and a working knowledge of the material is essential to do your job as a healthcare professional properly. In addition, we have tried to make studying for this exam as painless and as easy as possible. We have included all the essential information necessary for you to be successful on this exam. We have also included additional material to make studying this topic more fun and less painful.

We welcome your comments and suggestions. If you would like to offer a testimonial about how this book has helped you be successful, you will find more information about this at the end of the book.

We look forward to hearing from you. Good luck.
Joe & Michele Kunz
Long Island, New York

Part 1:
About ACLS

Notes

What Is The ACLS Certification Course All About?

1. Information About The Certification Class

The Advanced Cardiac Life Support programs are geared toward health professionals who work with victims and patients that may suddenly become acutely ill. The health professional may be dealing with the crisis as it starts or continues the care as the patient progresses or continues to need advanced care. The course prepares one for dealing with the patient in medical crisis and working with a highly credentialed team of life savers.

The participant is expected to come with knowledge and experience to the class. If this is limited there is ample study and reference materials, including study guides and youtube videos linked from Michelekunz.com. Preparation is key in the passing of ACLS and having a comfort level with the topics.

In the course there is a review of ECG's, medications, airway and circulation devices; defibrillators, monitors, pacemakers, AED's, Intraosseous (IO) needle placement, laryngeal mask airways (LMA's), intubation equipment and confirmation devices, simulation manikins, individual and team practice sessions, BLS and ACLS guidelines, and various recommendations, written, online, as well as practical exams.

The certification course requires preparation and time. If one is unsuccessful they will be rescheduled to retake the course at another time.

2. Information About The Exam

The exam is mutiple choice. It covers all the topics discussed and practiced in the certification program. There is time allotted for remediation and review of the exam questions whenever necessary. To prepare for the multiple choice test it is necessary to take the pretest. Bring any questions you have to class, or e-mail me any time at MKunz@MicheleKunz.com/.

3. Information About The Skills Station (Mega Code) Exam

The skills station enables the team to work together in the resuscitation of a patient. It also allows the team members of the class to participate in skills that their licensure or job description doesn't usually allow. Skills include ventilation, intubation, IO insertion, cardioversion, medication administration, etc. This helps the individuals on the team understand what the other team members are required to do, in priority and done properly.

The team will participate in a realistic simulation of a deteriorating patient where the team will initiate basic and advanced airways. The simulation will lead to IV/IO and fluid resuscitation and changes in the patient's ECG. Proper responses to the patient's change will require synchronized cardioversion (defibrillation/shock), intubation, intubation confirmation, capnography, intraosseous insertion, CPR, unsychronized cardioversion, trouble-shooting equipment failure, using the algorithms and and variations.

Each individual is responsible for understanding and performing in their assigned roles. The team will switch roles to ensure participation and team success. Team dynamics is a focus and ensures adequate communication among the resuscitation team members.

Each participant is required to have good BLS skills and to be able to demonstrate this at the time of the class. There is a review of BLS, AED use, and teamwork during the ACLS lecture and testing sessions. ACLS programs does not recertify the BLS requirements. BLS is a separate course with infant and children choking and CPR skills as well.

The team will review their actions in a debriefing to ensure the best treatment, interventions, and behaviors was applied, and to consider team members and family emotions during and after the critical event.

10 Hot Tips For Passing The ACLS Exam

Here is a guide to help you improve your chances of passing the certification exam for ACLS – Advanced Cardiac Life Support. If you take the advice given here seriously, you will do very well on the exam. But you must allow yourself plenty of time to learn all of this material – especially if you are new to this.

Tip # 1. Study And Memorize The *Zombie Notes Study Charts*

The *Zombie Notes Study Charts* focus on information from the literature, the test questions, and the real-life everyday situations - information you need to provide safe and effective care during an adult emergency or cardiac arrest. As you prepare for the course, try to memorize the medications and their doses. You must also memorize and understand the algorithms, the arrhythmias, and in which situations treatments and medications may be required.

Memorizing the algorithms, bradycardia – heart blocks and drug doses is the most difficult part. Repeating the information over and over, and even saying it aloud really helps with the memorization. Once the hard part is memorized, you can start using critical thinking in adjusting treatments based on patient symptoms. The *Zombie Notes* helps you study the need-to-know-information, and it is easy to take with you to study in your spare time.

Tip # 2. Read And Study The ECC Handbook

The American Heart Association textbook or the *ECC Handbook* may be distributed by your instructor. The ECC handbook is an excellent source for evidenced based treatment protocols for all age groups in emergency situations. It will assist the learner in identifying in priority the steps to take, meds to give, joules to use, essential equipment to have and post arrest recommendations to stabilize the patient.

This will help you in the mega code setting to apply your knowledge and skills. The handbook is filled with information of topics around assessing and treatment of critical situations, shock states, airway management, treatments and pharmacological modalities, for all age groups.

Tip # 3. Understand Basic ECG's

ACLS course focuses on the patient's heart rate and rhythm throughout the course. The treatments you select will be in response to your accurate choice of arrhythmia and if the patient is stable or unstable. Taking an ECG course is probably the most important preparation for ACLS class and testing. There are a variety of ways to take a course.

A classroom setting, an easy to understand textbook, or an online program are great options. YOU MUST be able to recognize and treat the lethal arrhythmias in the patient: ventricular fibrillation, ventricular tachycardia (with or without a pulse), pulseless electrical activity (PEA), and asystole. You will also need to recognize and treat unstable bradycardias and tachycardias, using medication, and a variety of emergency devices.

Tip # 4. Watch YouTube Videos On ECG And Other ACLS Topics

Any critically ill patient of any age may have their heart rate and rhythm affected. Trauma, age, medications, dehydration, heart failure, and heredity all play a part in a patient's arrhythmia. It is the practitioner's role to recognize potential cardiac changes and treat appropriately. Knowing the difference in synchronized and unsynchronized cardioversion (shock) is important. Other important rhythms to know are: bradycardia, and the 4 heart blocks; sinus tachycardia; and supraventricular tachycardia (SVT). You should be familiar with unusual arrythmias such as junctional and torsades de pointes.

Tip # 5. Take ACLS Practice Tests Over And Over Until You Get Every Question Correct

Practice tests can reinforce what you know and help you find the areas you need to focus your studies.

Tip # 6. Take A BLS Course And Be Sure You Can Perform High-Quality-CPR At The ACLS Class

The prerequisite to any Certification Course is the ability to perform BLS skills. The instructor may ask you for your card. During the ACLS course you will need to perform in practice and testing sessions. Some of the BLS skills will include: quick assessment for patient's response and pulse (10 seconds); chest compressions for adults; ventilations using a bag-mask-valve (Ambu bag); and the AED and application of AED pads.

Tip # 7. Review All The ACLS Medications And Their Doses

Oxygen, epinephrine, amiodarone, adenosine, atropine are the priority medications. Other drugs: antiarrythmic agents, beta blockers, and thrombolytic drugs are also discussed throughout the ACLS program. Lidocaine and procainamide are not the first line recommendation in the algorithms. In 2015 Vasopressin was removed from the cardiac arrest algorithm.

Tip # 8. Read About Different Diagnosis

Knowing the common diagnosis: dehydration, respiratory failure, septic and cardiogenic shock, trauma, etc., and the common treatments will ready you for the practice scenarios and testing mega (mock) code sessions. Identifying the symptoms and whether the patient is at risk for becoming unstable is key. When the systolic blood pressure is below 90 mm Hg, the patient is no longer considered stable.

While the patient is symptomatic but stable you must assess the patient and hope that a focused history and physical leads you to the current problem or diagnosis and appropriate treatments prior to the need for advanced life support measures. Prevention of cardiac arrest is the goal. This is where the Rapid Response Teams, and expert consultation is most appropriate.

This is when knowing and practicing the pneumonic "MOVIE" can be helpful as well. Put the patient on a "monitor", give them "oxygen" if needed, get the "vital signs", start a antecubital "IV" or IO, and obtain a 12-lead "ECG". The team is ready for any acute changes now. There are algorithms and guidelines to follow for the different diagnosis and arrythmias. Many are the standard of care nationally and world-wide - as in MI and stroke.

Treating shock and trauma involves many treatment protocols and medical disciplines to bring a patient to a stable condition. There are algorithms to assist the professionals in developing priorities around trauma: bradycardia, tachycardia, cardiac arrest, stroke, sepsis, and neurological assessments (Glascow Coma Scale), trauma and burns. Shock priorities include fluid replacement, electrolyte balance, vasoconstrictors, and temperature management (previously known as the hypothermia protocol), etc.

Tip # 9. Be Prepared To Work In A Team Setting And Be Able To Participate Verbally With Hands-On Participation

You may be assigned to a different role in the mega code. You may be practicing skills that your scope of practice does not allow in the real work place. The skills learned in the classroom allows you to see how we can help each other in an emergency situation. Feel free to speak up when the instructor allows team-work. Also be prepared to run a mega code as the team leader as well.

Tip # 10. Participate In Class, And Ask And Answer Lots Of Questions

Speaking up and asking many questions helps you understand and will facilitate your classrooms ask more detailed questions as well.

10 Hot Tips For Memorizing Information

Memorization is the fixing of information to your memory through sheer repetition. It is a necessary first step in learning. Memorization of essential terms and concepts of a difficult or new topic will provide a foundation for a deeper understanding that will follow with additional study. Michele and I teach thousands of healthcare professionals each year.

Everyone of them are expected to be able to quickly recall hundreds of essential dosages, formulas, and rules – all while under stress. Memorization, along with schooling, on-the-job training, conferences, and mandatory certifications, is an essential part of being a successful healthcare professional. Here is a list of our favorite ways to memorize a topic and its essential facts. Watch our YouTube video on this topic at YouTube.com/MicheleKunz.

Tip # 1: Break The Material Down Into Smaller Parts
Smaller bits of information will be much easier for your brain to hold onto. Make several lists. Work on memorizing these lists. Memorize a few facts, and them memorize a few more.

Tip # 2: Study In Short Periods Over A Long Period Of Time
Short burst of study, fifteen or thirty minutes at a time, are much better and more productive than sitting there and studying for sixty or ninety minutes. Whenever you are sitting somewhere, doctor's waiting room for example, take out your study cards and read them. These short busts of study periods can be very productive. Constantly doing this over many months is the surest way to get the information into your long-term memory.

Tip # 3: Review The Material Frequently
To get the new information from your short-term memory into your long-term memory you must review the material frequently. The more difficult the topic, and the less previous knowledge you have for a topic, the more frequently you must review the material. Some nights you will do a full study session of a subject. On the other nights you can do a quick review. But always try to touch upon that particular subject at least once every twenty-four hours.

Tip # 4: Do Not Cram

Cramming is usually useless. Learning a new or difficult topic takes time. Days, weeks, months, and years, not minutes. It takes a lot of time to process information properly.

Tip # 5: Use Mnemonics Devices And Catchy Puns And Phrases

Mnemonics are a great memory device to help your memorize difficult information. Here is one I created to remember the types of shock: "Not His lucky CHARMS", which stands for Neurogenic, Hemmorhagic, Cardiogenic, Hypovolemic, Anaphylactic, Respiratory, Metabolic, Septic.

Tip # 6: Teach The Information To Another Person

This is probably one of the surest ways to force yourself to thoroughly learn a topic. Get a family member or friend to sit and let you explain a topic to them. Have them ask you questions and put you on the spot for an answer that is understandable. Don't just talk at the person. Really try to help them understand the subject.

Forcing yourself to explain the topic to another person will force your brain to put the topic into a format that your brain is comfortable with. This will get you past simple memorization, and you will start to really learn a subject.

Tip # 7: Use Various Study Materials

This simply means using different study materials, such as flash-cards, videos, study guides, etc. One night you might use the flash-cards and videos. The next night use the textbook and your notes. Another night use the flash-cards and a study guide, and so on.

Tip # 8: Leave The Radio/TV Off

You must minimize outside distractions. You must study the material as intensely as possible, with all of your concentration abilities, for short busts of time. Your brain can easily handle two or three tasks at the same time. But when studying, especially a new subject, is not the time to distracted by other things.

Tip # 9: Use A Study Chart/Cards

Make your own study chart or flash cards. This is a great way to help you recognize what information that you are having difficulty with.

Tip # 10: Study With A Friend

This will certainly make studying a difficult subject much more fun. It will also be a great way to test each other. It is also a way to make sure that you will study instead of watching television.

10 Hot Tips for Surviving Your First Code

Here is a guide to help you, the healthcare professional, start to become a productive participant in an in-hospital emergency (code blue). Watch our YouTube video on this topic at YouTube.com/MicheleKunz.

Tip # 1: Call For Help Prior To A Cardiopulmonary Arrest Occurring

Yell down the hall for help, pick up the nearest phone, push the code button, and/or call the Rapid Response Team (RRT) or Medical Emergency Team (MET). Get help from your peers nearby as well as any code team or EMS that is on their way to help you. Call the team if you notice even subtle differences in the patient and their vital signs (including intractable pain). The RRT is to identify patient changes, have experts come to the bedside, and prevent clinical deterioration.

Tip # 2: Know The Emergency Number To Call

Post a sign with the number to call in an emergency with the name and address of your location if one would need to call EMS (911). In the hospital there may be a code number, a code button, intercom, RRT number, family RRT number. These numbers need to be memorized as well as clearly posted. When notifying the operator to page the team, be very clear with the location of the emergency, what type of emergency (cardiopulmonary arrest, Stroke code, Rapid Response Team, Security code, etc.).

Tip # 3: Stay Calm

When you know help is already on the way, you should be able to stay calm. Once you have called for help, the team and the equipment will be on the way. Getting yourself prepared for the worst emergency situation is also a great way to prepare your self. Decide what the worst thing that could happen to your patient could be, and decide what equipment you will most likely need. For example, if your patient is having trouble breathing, have an airway and bag-mask already in the room. If the IV is not running well, restart before an emergency occurs. Never leave your patient's side and work on the ABC's - airway, breathing, and circulation.

Tip # 4: Know How To Use Your Emergency Equipment

Before the emergency happens, you and your peers need to know where the emergency equipment is stored and how to use it properly. Know how to prepare the oxygen, suction and intubation equipment. Know what medications are in the code cart and what they are used for. This will help with your confidence in anticipating the patient's (and team) needs.

Tip # 5: Debriefing

Review the event afterwards to see what went well and what could have gone better. This includes the patient events and outcomes as well as how the team functioned together. Include the Pastoral Care or Social Work Department to help with emotional interventions for the family as well as meeting with staff members.

Tip # 6: Take Notes And Document Events

Document all vital signs (V/S), treatments, and decisions, during the event, with an exact timeline as best as possible during the event. You should keep your notes, especially if there could be a liability issue associated with the emergency situation.

Tip # 7: Certification And Review Courses

If you work in a procedural area, in a hospital, or medical facility, you probably should take a Basic Life Support (BLS) certification class. This class offers knowledge and skills regarding MI, stroke, chest compressions, Automatic External Defibrillator (AED), and airway adjuncts.

Another great class to take is the ECG Course. ACLS is an intense course with cardiac arrhythmias, emergency treatments, medications and cardiopulmonary arrest as a priority topic. 12-lead ECG classes are more advanced, but offers a better understanding of myocardial infarction and the implications for the patient, treatments, and outcomes. PALS and NRP are courses for pediatric and neonatal age groups. Advanced Trauma Life Support (ATLS) focuses on the treatments for trauma victims.

Tip # 8: Be Willing To Help Others

If there is an emergency in a patient area that you are not currently assigned to, you should be quick to offer assistance. In this type of situation you can learn and gain more experience. Assist, watch, listen, and learn. Be sure to know and work within your scope of practice.

Tip # 9: Know Your Patient

It is important to have all the patient's history, blood work with any test results, and any recent changes in the patient's status. Review the patient's medical record, listen carefully to the hand-off/report at the beginning of your shift. Do this before your hectic day begins. When the medical team arrives to the patient emergency they will have lots of questions about the patient. They will expect answers from you. Knowing these answers for the team allows for appropriate treatments, and perhaps faster and better patient outcomes.

Tip # 10: Post-Emergency Or Code

The period after the code has ended is also a stressful time. It is great if the code is successful and the patient survives. However, the patient may now need a higher lever of care, and need to be transferred to a critical care area. Time is needed to document the events and the patient outcomes. Of course, this is the time that everyone thinks the code is "over" and they all leave the room.

You need to make sure that the appropriate practitioners stay with you and the patient, ordering appropriate vasoactive infusions and medications while stabilizing and transporting the patient. If the patient does not survive the code, this is another time you don't want to be alone. You want another nurse, technician, or assistant to help with cleanup and preparing the body for a family viewing or transport to the morgue. Remember how you felt during this situation, and be there for your peers when it is their turn to respond to an emergency situation.

Top 10 AED Myths

There are many automatic external defibrillators (AED) available in medical facilities as well as public places. Most of the public know what an AED is - but have never had their hands on one or been trained on how to use one. And, because of this, many myths regarding AED use has developed. So, here is a list of the myths that Michele and I hear the most often from our healthcare students as well as the general public.

Myth # 1: AED's Are Difficult To Use

No. After you have called the emergency response team (Code "Blue" or 911) and you have begun CPR on a victim who appears pulseless and breathless, ask a bystander to get the AED. When an AED is available, simply turn it on and follow the AED's prompts. The AED's are easy to use and are highly accurate in determining if defibrillation (shock) is needed. The AED talks and prompts you through the correct and safe use of the pads. "Apply pads to patient's bare chest and plug in the connector". It is easier if one person can do the chest compressions while the other applies the AED pads. Anyone who has taken a CPR class learns about the AED and how to use it. Nothing difficult about it. If it is not working – just do chest compressions.

Myth # 2: If I Put The Pads On Wrong I Will Get Sued

No. The AED pads have pictures on the pads that explain where to apply the pads. If the pads aren't placed properly, the AED may ask you to correct their placement. If the AED cannot analyze or does not find a shockable rhythm, you will go back to high quality chest compressions. Even if the victim is lying in snow, you can use an AED. The chest needs to be dry enough that the pads will stick.

We don't know of any lawsuits that have been brought against lay rescuers who attempt to provide CPR and use an AED. Generally speaking, our legal system provides nationwide Good Samaritan protection, exempting anyone who renders emergency treatment (outside the hospital setting) in an effort to save someone's life. Laws suits are usually focused around health clubs or similar institutions that have employees that did not have or use an AED at the time of a cardiac arrest.

Myth # 3: It Is Too Late To Deliver A Shock After 2 Minutes Of CPR

No, it is not too late. A rescuer must deliver, and continue to deliver, high quality CPR. When the AED does arrive and the pads are applied to the victim, the AED will determine if the victim is still in a shockable rhythm, and it will tell you to press the shock button. There is still a chance of survival.

Myth # 4: AED's Pads Are Not Interchangeable For Different Age Groups

Wrong. The AED pads are made for the specific age groups – one size for adults, and another for children, and still another for infants. But, of course, the most common age group for AED usage is the older adult. Adult pads can be used on the child 1 to 8 years old, and even on infants, if the correct size is not available. The pads will need to be placed on the front and back, avoiding the pads touching each other. Infant/child combo pads are available for use as well. Do not use smaller pads on adults, because it will not provide enough joules (electrical power). In this case, continue applying chest compressions – high quality CPR. What is not interchangeable – is the brand or manufacturer of the pads. Use the brand of pads that is made for the AED that you have.

Myth # 5: The Chest Must Be Dry In Order For The AED Pads To Work

Wrong. Obviously the chest should be as dry as possible for the strongest and safest delivery of a shock. If possible, quickly dry off the chest, but do not delay defibrillation if the AED suggests a shock is required. A hairy chest can actually interefere with the pads sticking and giving an effective shock.

Myth # 6: Do Not Use The AED If The Victim Has A Pacemaker/Defibrillator, Medication Patch, Or Is In Contact With A Metal Surface

Wrong. If there is an apparent device under the skin where the pads would be placed, simply place the pads in another spot at least 2 inches away from the device. Remove any medication patch and dry the area. If you think the victim is being shocked by their own internal defibrillator, stand clear. Be prepared to start CPR and apply the AED pads as well. Call 911 as soon as possible. It has been proven that moving patients off of metal surfaces is unnecessary because there is very little risk to the CPR provider as long as they are not touching the victim when the shock is delivered.

Myth # 7: AED's Malfunction And Don't Give Enough Joules

Wrong. The number of AED malfunctions is very small compared to the number of the times AEDs are used without a problem. AEDs recognize shockable arrhythmias and can deliver up to 360 joules, based on the model. Data shows approximately 325,000 deaths annually due to sudden cardiac arrest (SCA) and that many of these lives could possibly be saved with the quick and proper use of and AED.

Myth # 8: Home AED's Do Not Save Lives

Approximately 80% of the deaths occur in the home, so it makes sense to have an AED in the home. However, family members often do not remember where the AED is located within their own home or within in their parent's home. Family members are also afraid to use it once the find the AED. They typically fear that they will use it incorrectly and harm their loved one. If the AED is used quickly and correctly, it can save a life. We must remember that AED's are very often used successfully in major public locations like shopping malls, airports, and casinos.

Myth # 9: I Need To Be A Healthcare Professional To Use The AED

Wrong. Certainly, if you are a health professional and use emergency equipment every day you would probably be comfortable using an AED - applying the pads and actually shocking someone. But the AED is so simple and straight forward to use that anyone in the general public can use successfully – even without taking a CPR certification class. But there are classes for the general public that include AED training.

Myth # 10: There Are No Resources For The Lifesaver In The Community

Wrong. There are plenty of life-saver and CPR classes in schools, libraries, community centers, and hospitals throughout America. There are also plenty of very good free videos on YouTube. The American Heart Association (AHA) sells a video with an inexpensive blow-up manikin to help a family practice their CPR skills. There are also applications for smart-phones that can help you call the 911, as well as guide you through the steps of CPR. There are also applications that alert CPR providers of emergency cardiac arrest calls that are close to their location.

Top 10 CPR Myths

Michele and I have been teaching CPR to healthcare professionals and students since 1984. We have seen the development, improvement, and wide-spread acceptance of CPR education over these years. Despite these advances, we still hear many myths about CPR every time we teach a class. As healthcare professionals and students, we must not allow old information, nor the public's misperceptions and fears about CPR, nor Hollywood's unrealistic depiction of CPR, to affect our duty to provide high-quality CPR to our patients and to the public. Therefore, in order to help dispel these myths, Michele and I have created this list of the most common CPR myths that we hear the most often from the healthcare professionals and students that we teach every day.

Myth # 1: CPR Must Include Mouth-To-Mouth Breathing

Wrong. Health professionals or first responders will initiate chest compressions immediately. The breaths should be done preferably with a bag mask, mouth to mask or mouth to mouth with a barrier device. If you do not have a barrier device or CPR face-mask, you can perform continuous chest compressions without ventilations until emergency services arrives. The American Heart Association has revised its recommendations and encouraged lay bystander rescuers to use "hands-only" CPR as an alternative to CPR with exchange of breaths.

Myth # 2: CPR Always Works

Wrong. Unfortunately, this is not true, and is a very common belief that has been perpetuated by Hollywood. The actual adult survival rate from out-of-hospital cardiac arrest is about 2% to 15%. Survival rates can increase up to 30% if an AED is used to deliver a shock. However, if the victim's heart stops and no one starts CPR immediately - then the victim's chance of survival is zero.

Myth # 3: I Could Get Sued If I Administer CPR In The Wrong Way Or Make A Mistake

Wrong. We have not read of any successful lawsuits that have been brought against lay rescuers or healthcare professionals who attempt to provide CPR. Generally speaking, our legal system provides nationwide Good Samaritan protection, exempting anyone who renders emergency treatment outside the hospital setting, with CPR in an effort to save someone's life. This includes lay rescuers and healthcare professionals. Lawsuits are usually focused around health clubs or similar institutions that have employees that did not have or use an AED at the time of a cardiac arrest. Generally, as long as lay rescuers and healthcare professionals do not waver too far from standard CPR procedure, they will most likely be protected.

Myth # 4: We Can Become Proficient In CPR With An Online Class

Wrong. While it is true that you can learn the steps of CPR from an on-line class, you most likely would not be able to perform high-quality CPR on a real patient after taking a computer based CPR class. Hands-on practice, with the guidance of a certified instructor, is the key to developing muscle memory and proper techniques.

Myth # 5: We Can Save A Sudden Cardiac Arrest Victim With CPR Alone

Wrong. An AED/defibrillator can deliver shocks that will return the fibrillating heart to its normal rhythm. In most cases, CPR alone cannot revive a sudden cardiac arrest victim. CPR can delay death until a defibrillator delivers a lifesaving shock.

Myth # 6: A Patient Should Cough While Having A Heart Attack To Prevent The Heart Attack From Getting Worse

Wrong. This myth is what is known as 'Cough CPR'. Cough CPR was thought to speed up a very slow heart rate (bradycardia) and keep the patient conscious till emergency services arrived. It is probably a misinterpretation of the vagal maneuver. The vagal maneuver is used to help a patient stimulate the vagus nerve to slow down a fast heart rate.

Myth # 7: Cardiac Arrest Is The Same As A Heart Attack

Wrong. They are different conditions and are treated differently. Cardiac arrest is caused by an arrhythmia, dysrhythmia, electrolyte imbalance and trauma, which can lead to cardiac standstill, where the heart is not moving (asystole) or is fibrillating. A heart attack is a myocardial infarction, caused by a blocked coronary artery (acute coronary syndrome). Therefore, the term 'cardiac arrest' is not synonymous with 'heart attack'.

A patient experiencing a heart attack may experience chest pain, nausea, vomiting, and become diaphoretic. However, a heart attack may ultimately lead to cardiac arrest depending on the severity of the blockage in the heart.

Myth # 8: Someone With More Experience Than Me Should Help The Victim, So I Shouldn't Help

Wrong. The key to surviving cardiac arrest is the immediate response of someone trained in CPR. A patient who collapses and does not immediately receive chest compressions has little or no chance of survival. If you know how to do chest compressions properly you should help immediately. Call for EMS initially then start chest compressions on the lower half of the breastbone.

Myth # 9: CPR Can Do More Harm Than Good

Wrong. When you are performing CPR it is on someone who has no heartbeat. Proper chest compressions, to be effective, must be fast and very hard. It is true that you may possibly break some of the victim's ribs while performing CPR. Once a victim is resuscitated injuries can be treated. Damaged ribs are worth the risk and much better than letting the victim die without attempting to give CPR. Ambulance personnel utilize a "thumper" device which uses a piston and plunger device, which is battery operated, to does continuous chest compressions for lengthy period of times. Ribs may break with this device, however you can survive rib fractures.

Myth # 10: CPR Will Always Re-Start The Victim's Heart If They Are In Asystole

Wrong. CPR alone will not always re-start a heart that is not beating. The purpose of administering CPR is to push oxygenated blood to the victim's heart and vital organs. Continuing high-quality CPR increases your chance of survival with a defibrillation when indicated. Emergency medications such as epinephrine may assist in getting the blood flow back into the heart and other vital organs (kidneys and brain).

Popular Code Drugs and Emergency Medications

There are about five emergency drugs that you will need to know as a health professional. If you work in the hospital, procedure area, or are a member of an emergency response team, these are the drugs that you need to have readily available and know when to use, how much to give, and how to give.

1. Epinephrine: is usually considered the first line medication in cardiac arrest. Epinephrine (adrenalin) is a hormone-neurotransmitter, that causes stimulation and increase in heart rate and vasoconstriction. It is readily available in the code cart in a 1 mg, 10 ml syringe. The dose of Epinephrine is 1 mg every 3 to 5 minutes, with no maximum dose. It is used in cardiac arrest as an IV push medication. It can also be used as an infusion in an unstable patient that needs their heart rate and blood pressure increased. Epinephrine infusion dosing is 0.1 to 0.5 mcg/kg/min.

2. Amiodarone: this is a popular antiarrhythmic medication. During cardiac arrest after epinephrine it is first line antiarrhythmic recommended. The dose during cardiac arrest is 300 mg IVP. This can be repeated one at 150 mg IVP. When the patient has a fast atrial or ventricular tachycardia, with a pulse, amiodarone is given over 10 minutes, due to the hypotensive side effects. The dose is 150 mg in 100 ml, over 10 minutes.

3. Atropine: is not considered a "code" drug. It is used for symptomatic and unstable bradycardia patients when the heart rate is slow, usually below 50 bpm. The dose of atropine is 0.5 mg IVP every 3 to 5 minutes with a maximum does of 3 mg. It is usually available in 1 mg prefilled (10 ml) syringes in the code cart (use 5 ml at a time). In patients with a heart blocks (2nd degree, type II and 3rd degree) atropine may be ineffective. Transcutaneous pacemaker and Dopamine are the next recommended treatments for unstable bradycardia. Epinephrine infusion is a last resort for the patient who most likely is having myocardial ischemia.

4. Adenosine: is a fast acting drug used for supraventricular tachycardia and Wolff-Parkinson-White Syndrome (WPW). It causes dramatic side effects, when given IVP. Administer in the IV line as close to the heart as possible, and be sure to flush it in quickly with 10 to 20 ml of normal saline. Expect to see flat line on the cardiac monitor when this medication works.

It then causes temporary ischemic chest pain, and other related symptoms. The half-life and these dramatic symptoms last only 6 seconds. The initial dose of adenosine is 6 mg, and then repeat, with a second dose of 12 mg IVP. This drug is used in SVT after the vagal maneuvers were unsuccessful. Synchronized cardioversion and amiodarone are given if initial treatment does not work to slow the heart rate down.

5. Lidocaine And Procainamide: are alternative antiarrythmic agents, especially if it has worked for the patient to reduce ventricular arrythmias, in the past, or amiodarone has not been effective.

Cardiac and Vasoactive Medication Basics

Listed below are commonly used medications, used for medical conditions including hypertension and tachy-arrythmias. All healthcare providers should know these medications and the actions, side-effects, and the potential interactions they can have with other medications. The medications below are used on a daily basis, mostly in an oral preparations.

1. Beta-Blockers: or beta-adrenergic blocking agent is used to treat cardiac arrhythmias and protect form myocardial infarctions. B1 selective blocker medications slow down the heart rate and causes vasodilation which lowers the blood pressure. The most common of these beta-blockers are Atenolol (Tenormin), nebivolol (Bystolic), esmolol (Brevibloc), carvedilol (Coreg), Metoprolol (Lopressor, Toprol), bisoprolol (Zabeta, Monocor), and betapase (Sotolol).

In choosing the appropriate beta-blockers, a prescriber can target specific B1 or B2. B1 blocker is the most popular. B2 adrenergic blockers act on smooth muscle, thus causing bronchoconstriction. This is not helpful in patients with asthma and COPD. This is why medications that cause B2 to be blocked are not used on patients with pulmonary disease history.

2. Calcium Channel Blocker: is a popular drug to treat Atrial Fibrillation, and Atrial Flutter. This medication decreases the heart rate and causes vasodilation to reduce the blood pressure. As a negative inotropic drug it reduces the force of myocardial contraction. As a negative chronotropic medication, it reduces the heart rate. Some of the popular calcium channel blockers used to treat hypertension and arrhythmias today are: diltiazem (Cardiazem), verapamil (Calan), amlodipine (Norvasc), nifedipine (Procardia), and nicardipine (Cardene).

3. ACE Inhibitors: angiotensive converting enzyme inhibitor. These medications inhibit the angiotensin I enzyme to convert to angiotensin II via the renin system which usually causes blood vessels to constrict, thus vasodilation results with reduction in blood pressure. Popular names are enalapril (Vasotec), captopril (Capoten), lisinopril (Prinivil, Zestril), and quinapril (Accupril). They are often prescribed for hypertension, congestive heart failure, and to improve survival from a heart attack. Always teach your patients about angioedema.

A cough and swelling of the lips and/or airway are signs of angioedema. This is an allergic reaction, which can be mild, but can lead to serious and fatal outcomes if not treated. The ACE inhibitor prescription can be changed to an angiotensin II receptor blocker (ARB) or other antihypertensive medication. A reaction like this usually occurs within a few days or weeks of starting therapy, but may not appear for months or years later. There is a higher risk of angioedema swelling in the African American population taking this drug.

4. ACE Receptor Inhibitors (ARB's): angiotensive converting enzyme receptor inhibitor. These medications are used to treat hypertension and congestive heart failure, and are rarely associated with the persistant cough/angioedema caused by ACE Inhibitors. Popular ARBS are: losartan (Cozaar), valsartan (Diovan), and irbesartan (Avapro).

Many of these medications are combined with a diuretic (hydrochlorothiazide) to treat hypertension and congestive heart failure.

Arrhythmia Basics For Healthcare Professionals

Arrhythmias are usually caused by stimulation or irritability of the heart muscle. It can simply be a fast or slow heart rate, or a dangerous irregular rhythm caused by ectopic foci. When there are irritable spots or ectopic foci in any area of the heart muscle it can cause disruption of the normal electrical cycle. These extra beats do conduct through parts or down through to the ventricles. This disturbance can be considered normal, but can also put a person at risk for chaotic arrhythmias that can give one chest pressure, discomfort, and lead to unstable, (hopefully) treatable arrhythmias, and at worst - cardiac arrest.

All health professionals need to recognize the signs and symptoms of arrhythmias and be ready to call a team that can provide life-saving measures: such as medications, chest compressions, synchronized cardioversion and defibrillation. The three most common arrhythmias originate from the atrium, atrial-ventricular (AV) node and ventricles.

A. Arrhythmias That Originate In The Atria

1. Sinus Tachycardia: the sinus node sends out electrical signals faster than usual. Anxiety, pain, asthma medications and dehydration/hypovolemia are common causes of a fast heart rate (above 100 bpm, below 150).

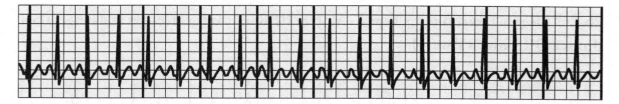

2. Sinus Bradycardia: the sinus node sends out electrical signals slower (less than 60) than usual. Slow rates can be in normal in athletic and older healthy individuals. Medications are often given to prevent their heart rate from speeding up. After a myocardial infarction, the electrical conduction patterns may be damaged and lead to other slow dangerous rhythms called heart blocks. Symptomatic bradycardia is usually caused by one of the heart blocks, where conduction through the myocardium is disturbed.

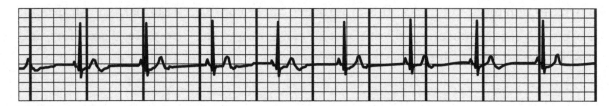

2a. 1st Degree Heart Block (PR interval consistently prolonged more than 0.20 seconds)

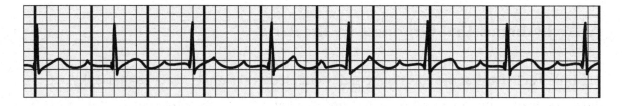

2b. 2nd Degree Heart Block - Type I - Mobitz I (PR interval gets longer and longer then drops a QRS after a P wave)

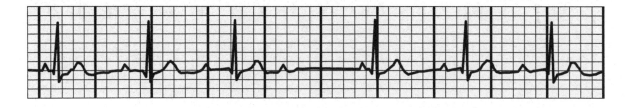

2c. 2nd Degree Heart Block - Type II - Mobitz II (more P's than Q's, but everytime there is a QRS there is a consistent PR interval.)

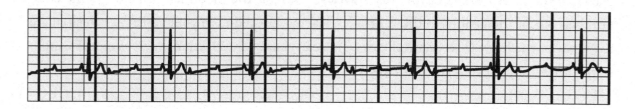

2d. 3rd Degree Heart Block - Complete Heart Block - AV Dissociation (more P's than Q's, without any relationship). The atrium and ventricals are working independently of each other, and often inefficiently.

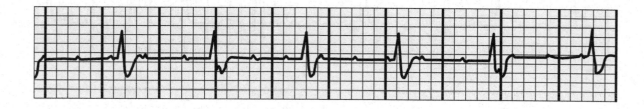

3. Premature Atrial Contraction (PAC's): premature atrial contractions are the most common cause of irregular heart rates. The early beat that initiates from an irritable foci in the atrium, causes the irregular rhythm. Palpitations may be felt, but it does not cause the patient to become unstable. Menopausal woman often experience PAC's. Treatment includes the reduction of stimulants like coffee and chocolate. Medications like beta-blockers are often effective.

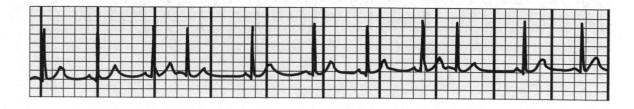

4. Atrial Fibrillation: in atrial fibrillation, the electrical activity originates from numerous abnormal electrical foci in the atrium, causing the atria to fibrillate or quiver. Notice the very wavy baseline with many fibrillatory waves (F-waves). The blood is not getting efficiently pumped out of the atrium to the ventricles, leaving less blood in your ventricles to circulate throughout the body (loss of atrial kick). This can cause complications such as clots forming in the atria, which can lead to strokes and TIA's (transient ischemic attacks).

The treatment for atrial fibrillation is medications, and/or a procedure called ablation therapy, which will eliminate the extra conduction patterns in the heart tissue. If the heart rate is rapid and V/S unstable, synchronized cardioversion is the treatment.

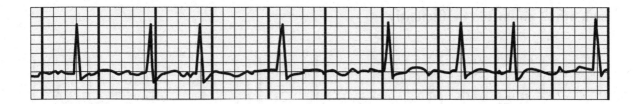

5. Atrial Flutter: atrial flutter is one irritable foci firing rapidly in the atrium causing the atrium of the heart to quiver as in atrial fibrillation. Notice the course "F" (fibrillatory) waves in the baseline. This is called the saw-tooth or picket fence baseline. The treatment is medications and synchronized cardioversion, if unstable. A procedure called ablation therapy may eliminate the extra conduction patterns in the heart tissue.

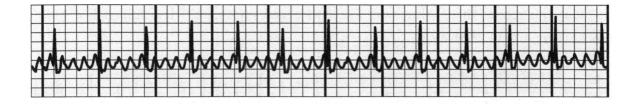

6. Supraventricular Tachycardia (SVT): this is a very fast heart rate originating in the upper part of the heart muscle, above the ventricles. The heart rate is over 150 beats per minute. This can cause many symptoms including low blood pressure (hypotension) and dizziness. Medications are used to slow the heart rate down. If medications are unsuccessful, synchronized cardioversion is a procedure where the heart is shocked (cardioverted). This causes the heart to stop and restart itself back into a regular rhythm. Ablation therapy is also a treatment to eradicate the extra abnormal conduction patterns in the heart.

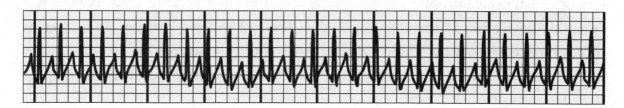

7. Wolff-Parkinson-White Syndrome: this is a rare rapid arrhythmia. There are extra pathways between the atrium and the ventricles (Bundle of Kent) where the electricity is conducted rapidly through the heart. This extra accessory pathway can lead to rapid heart rates. There is a delta wave, (see arrow) which is a slurred upstroke in the QRS. There is also a shorter PR interval. Treatment includes medication and or ablation therapy.

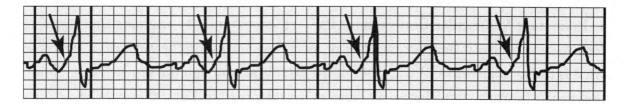

B. Arrhythmias Originating In The AV Node

1. Junctional (Nodal) Rhythm: the Atrioventricular (AV) node becomes the pacemaker when the sinus node is not functioning (after anesthesia, a myocardial infarction, or when the AV node becomes an irritable foci). These beats go through the normal ventricular electrical conduction patterns, thus there are narrow QRS's, and the cardiac output is usually adequate. When the AV node fires, it also sends the electricity up to the atrium through existing conduction patterns, causing the atrium to depolarize. These P waves will be upside-down, called retrograde conduction. The upside-down P waves can be present before, hidden, or after the QRS. The heart rate is usually between 40 to 60 bpm but can be as fast as 180 bpm. In the picture below the P waves cannot be seen, becasuse they are buried in the QRS.

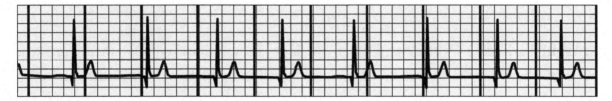

C. Arrhythmias Originating In The Ventricles

1. Premature Ventricular Contraction (PVC): these extra beats originate from irritable foci in the ventricle. If there are mulitple, or more than one foci in the ventricle, it can cause what is called multi-focal PVC's. It sends the extra beats through the ventricles disrupting the regular heart rhythm. These may cause an irregular rhythm, but if this extra beat occurs at the same time the heart muscle is repolarizing (on the T wave) it can result in a life-threatening arrhythmia called ventricular fibrillation or ventricular tachycardia. The heart does not pump efficiently and CPR will be needed. This "R on T" phenomenon, is often called "sudden death", where the AED (automatic external defibrillator) will be useful.

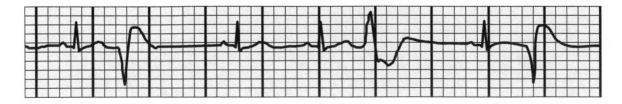

2. Ventricular Fibrillation: or sudden death is when the heart fibrillates and there isn't any normal pumping. Chest compressions are started and the patient will need defibrillation, which can save their life. Patients who survive this should have an ICD (Implanted Cardioverter Defibrillator) inserted.

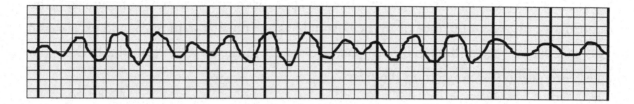

3. Ventricular Tachycardia: if there is a pulse, the treatment is medication and immediate cardioversion. This individual will need and an ICD (Implanted Cardioverter Defibrillator) to prevent future cardiac arrests. In Ventricular Tachycardia (V-Tach) the patient may have a pulse, and require antiarrythmic medications and synchronized cardioversion. But if they lose their pulse, this is considered a deadly arrhythmia, and CPR must be started. Unsynchronized cardioversion (defibrillation) is needed immediately. This picture is of Monomorphic Ventricular Tachycardia (VT).

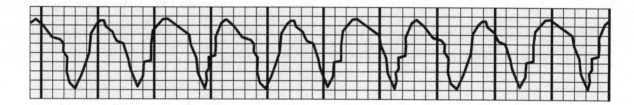

4. Torsade's dePointes: is a rare rapid ventricular rhythm caused by hypomagnesemia and hypokalemia (electrolyte imbalances), and certain medications. It is the Polymorphic form of ventricular tachycardia and can be deadly as well, especially if the patient loses their pulse. Magnesium, antiarrythmics, and cardioversion treatments are needed immediately.

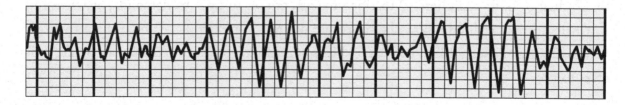

How A Pacemaker Works

Pacemakers can be life-savers when the heart rate becomes so slow that the patient may become light-headed, unstable, and have very low blood pressure. There are 3 different types of pacemakers. In an emergency there is a need for the transcutaneous pacemaker. The defibrillator on the ambulance or in the hospital has a defibrillator/monitor and pacemaker. The pacemaker (defibrillator-combo) pads are placed in the front and on the back of the chest often called "sandwiching the heart".

The pads are then cabled to a monitor/defibrillator. Settings are selected; heart rate, fixed or demand response, and current (measured in milliamps). The current is increased until electrical capture - a spike and a QRS is seen on the cardiac monitor. Target rate is generally set between 60 to 80 bpm.

The cardiologist may start the pacemaker at 10 milliamps and increase by increments of 10 until capture is noted. Strongly consider sedation, as external pacing can be quite uncomfortable. Most patients cannot tolerate currents of 50 milliamps and higher, without sedation. If continued pacing is required the medical team should insert the transvenous pacemaker, through a central line into the heart. Once the patient is stabilized, the decision to implant a permanent pacemaker device would be made.

The transvenous pacemaker usually has two leads which provide pacing and sensing activity for the atrium and/or ventricle wires. In an emergency it is usually a ventricular pacemaker wire that is inserted. Pacemakers are classified using three or more letters, which describe the functions of the pacemaker. These functions include which chambers are sensed, which chambers are potentially paced, and if the pacer is inhibited by sensing the heart beating.

The first letter identifies what chamber is paced. The letter can be A (atrial), V (ventricular) or D (dual or both chambers). Most pacemakers are set to fire on "demand", or when the intrinsic heart rate slows below the heart rate desired. For example, if the heart rate drops below the pacemaker setting, such as 50 beats per minute, for example, the pacemaker will start to fire.

The second letter identifies what chamber is sensed. Like the paced chamber, A represents atrial sensing, V represents ventricular sensing, and D represents dual (identifies a pacemaker that has the ability to sense both chambers).

The third letter represents the pacemaker activity in the specific chambers. The letters I (inhibited) and T (triggered) are used for the third letter, based on the heart beat being sensed or not. For the transvenous pacemaker wires, less milliamps (10 to 20 milliamps) (as compared to the transcutaneous pacemaker) are needed, because they are directly stimulating the ventricular wall.

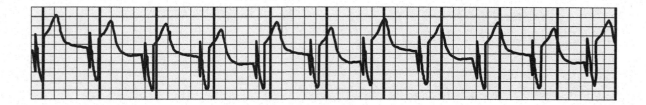

Examples:
VVI = Ventricle paced; ventricle sensed; pacing inhibited if beat sensed.
DDD = Atrium and ventricle can both be paced; atrium and ventricle both sensed; pacing triggered in each chamber if beat not sensed.

The pacer electrodes also sense the electrical activity at the myocardial surface. The sensitivity of a pacemaker is the minimum voltage required to "see" or detect a P wave or R (QRS) wave, measured in mV. The sensitivity of the pacemaker is a setting on the pacemaker device, where the lower the number, the more sensitive the pacemaker. The range of sensitivity for a pacemaker is 0.4 to 10mV for the atria, and 0.8 to 20mV for the ventricles.

When the pacemaker is working properly the ECG picture will display a "spike", which is a vertical line. This is the pacemaker firing. The usually wide QRS following the spike is called the "capture". This means the heart wall is sensitive to the pacer firing and electrical activity is effective. Hopefully the cardiac output is sufficient and the patient's heart rate and blood pressure will normalize.

Notes

Part 2:
The Questions

Notes

Certification Exam Practice Questions For ACLS

1. When a victim has and advanced airway inserted (intubated) what is the recommended method for performing high-quality CPR?

a. 30:2 compressions to ventilations ratio

b. 15:2 compressions to ventilations ratio

c. 5:1 compressions to ventilations ratio

d. Continuous chest compressions with 10 ventilations per minute

2. While you are taking your patient's blood pressure, the patient gasps and loses consciousness. After calling for help and determining that the patient is not breathing, you cannot palpate the pulse within 10 seconds. What is your next action?

a. Begin chest compressions

b. Run down the hall to get the code cart

c. Give a precordial thump

d. Turn the patient on their side

3. What is the advantage of using quantitative waveform capnography during cardiac arrest?

a. Measures the pulse oximetry levels

b. Measures oxygen levels via the nasal cannula

c. Allows for monitoring of CPR quality and measures expired carbon dioxide

d. Determines the amount of sodium bicarbonate that will be needed

4. The Emergency Department (ED) team is attempting to resuscitate a victim who was brought into the ED in Ventricular Fibrillation (V-Fib) with CPR in progress. The ED staff delivered 4 shocks, 3 doses of epinephrine, amiodarone 300 mg, 2 liters of normal saline, and the victim converted to asystole, which persists despite and high-quality CPR. What is your next consideration?

a. Discuss with the team, terminating the resuscitative efforts

b. Look for the DNR order

c. 1 mg of atropine

d. Vasopressin 20 units

5. The team is treating a cardiac arrest victim. The patient is intubated, a peripheral antecubital IV is inserted and continuous chest compressions are performed. Minutes later you reassess the waveform on the capnography screen and a PETCO2 level of 6 mm Hg is displayed. What does a PETCO2 of less than 10 mm Hg signify to the team?

a. The patient meets the criteria for termination of efforts

b. The endotracheal tube is no longer in the trachea

c. Chest compressions may not be effective

d. The team is ventilating the patient too often (hyperventilation)

6. Prior to delivering a defibrillation (shock) to a patient you must first . . . ?

a. Check for a pulse before and after the shock

b. Place a non-rebreather on the victims face

c. Be sure "oxygen flow is clear" from patient's chest

d. Stop the compressions 30 seconds prior to the "all clear" warning

7. What is the depth of compressions for adults in cardiac arrest?

a. 1/2 to 1 inch

b. 2 to 2-1/2 inches

c. 3 inches - at least

d. Only ventilations are recommended

8. How can the team minimize any interruptions during CPR to less than 10 seconds?

a. Deliver IV medications only when an intraosseous is inserted

b. Have someone count out-loud

c. Continue CPR while charging the defibrillator, and resume immediately after the shock

d. Perform pulse checks immediately before and after defibrillation

9. What action besides starting chest compressions is extremely important in the Basic Life Support Survey?

a. Obtaining the blood sugar result

b. Early defibrillation with an AED

c. Hypothermia protocol

d. Epinephrine administration

10. The team is continuing resuscitation efforts in the doctor's office. After a shock of 200 J the patient remains in ventricular fibrillation. CPR is continued for two minutes, epinephrine 1 mg IV push given. What is the next treatment recommended?

a. Sotalol 200 mg IV slowly

b. Defibrillation at 360 J

c. Amiodarone 150 mg over 10 minutes

d. Procainamide 20 mg/kg per minute

11. When using continuous capnography, what evidence is a sign of ineffective chest compressions?
a. A dampened waveform
b. Loud beeps
c. PETCO2 < 10 mm Hg
d. PETCO2 > 100 mm Hg

12. What is the recommended maximum time period for pausing in chest compressions?
a. Up to twenty (20) seconds
b. Ten (10) seconds or less
c. Less than five (5) seconds
d. Interruptions are always acceptable

13. Why is the rapid response team (RRT) summoned to the patient's room?
a. To quicken the admission process through the emergency department
b. To take the place of the anesthesiologist if intubation is needed
c. To assist the existing team in identifying the problem and preventing further deterioration
d. To treat patients outside the hospital patient care areas only

14. Which of the following actions is done first to restore circulation, oxygenation and ventilation to unresponsive pulseless victims?
a. Providing advanced interventions despite interruptions in CPR
b. Obtaining a 12-lead ECG and chest X-Ray
c. Obtaining an arterial blood gas
d. High quality CPR

15. Which of the following will enhance the quality of chest compressions during cardiac arrest situations?

a. Pausing every 5 cycles to decrease the possibility of exhaustion

b. Compress at the rate of 80 to 100 compressions per minute

c. Switch providers about every 2 minutes or every 5 cycles

d. Compress the upper half of the sternum

16. You are caring for an adult victim in respiratory failure. The patient is attempting to breath independently. There is a strong pulse but you must assist with ventilations. What is the recommended rate of assisting ventilations with a bag-valve-mask device for this patient?

a. 1 breath every 5 to 6 seconds

b. 1 breath every 3 to 5 seconds

c. 2 breaths every 6 to 8 seconds

d. 2 breaths every 3 to 5 seconds

17. You are receiving a patient into the Emergency Department who has positive signs and symptoms of a stroke. You realize this diagnosis is disabling and has a high risk of mortality. What is the initial plan for this patient when they arrive to the ED?

a. The patient needs a non-contrast CAT scan within 25 minutes of arrival

b. Schedule the patient for aggressive rehabilitation therapy

c. Make sure the neurologist sees the patient on rounds

d. Lower the patient's blood pressure to 90 systolic in order to give the IV fibrinolytics rtPA (recombinant tissue plasminogen activator)

18. A paramedic is evaluating a 67-year-old man. Upon interview of the patient they recognize slurred and slowing of the man's speech. The blood pressure of 180/98 mm Hg, a heart rate of 96/minute, a non-labored respiratory rate of 20 breaths/minute, and a pulse oximetry reading of 98%. The ECG displays sinus rhythm. What action would be performed next?

a. 100% supplementary oxygen

b. A Pre-hospital Stroke Scale, and notify the ED

c. Retrieve a guaiac specimen

d. IV rtPA immediately (intravenous recombinant tissue plasminogen activator)

19. Prior to the arrival of the stroke patient to the ED, the Radiology Department calls you with the news that the CAT scanner is not working temporarily, and that repairs are being made. What should you do in this situation?

a. Have the patient come and wait for the repairs to be completed

b. Ensure a safe disposition and divert the ambulance to a nearby hospital if possible

c. Close the ED until repairs are made

d. Have the patient take an aspirin and come back in the morning

20. You arrive in minutes to a Rapid Response Team call for a patient who has a change in mental status and right arm weakness. The team initially obtained a blood pressure of 188/110 mm Hg, the pulse rate is 90/minute, the respiratory rate is 14 breaths/ minute, and the pulse oximetry reading is 93% on room air. The lead II ECG displays sinus rhythm. The blood glucose level is within normal limits. What intervention should be done next?

a. Administer 100% oxygen

b. Administration of an epinephrine infusion

c. Transfer to the rehab unit

d. Head CT scan

21. You are participating in a rescue mission. The death toll is rising. Your team is searching the area for survivors. When finding victims when would it be inappropriate to initiate or continue chest compressions?

a. There are signs of rigor mortis and post-mortem lividity

b. The arrest was not witnessed

c. No return of spontaneous circulation after 2 minutes of CPR

d. Patient appears to be very old

22. Your 68-year-old patient, Mrs. Sandy Cheeks, who has emphysema, is in the telemetry unit. She is complaining of dizziness and fatigue. The patient's heart rate is 40 bpm, the blood pressure is 96/54 mm Hg, and the respiratory rate is 18 breaths/minute. The oxygen saturation remains unchanged at 94%. What is the appropriate first medication?

a. Epinephrine 1 mg

b. Hypoxia exists and use a non-rebreather device at 15 L/minute

c. A focused assessment, 12-lead ECG, and consider Atropine 0.5 mg

d. Tachy-arrhythmia exists and administer Adenosine 6 mg IVP fast and flush

23. Mrs. Cheek's initial atropine doses were ineffective, and the physician requests an infusion. Her blood pressure is now 84/50. She is responding to your commands, and is OK with laying flat in her bed. What is an appropriate medicated infusion for this patient?

a. Dopamine 2 to 10 mcg/kg per minute

b. Dopamine 2 to 10 mg/minute

c. Epinephrine 10 to 15 mg/minute

d. Epinephrine 10 to 15 meq/kg per minute

24. Mr. Sheldon J. Plankton, age 89, rings his call bell and complains of palpitations. The patient's heart rate is 172 minute, blood pressure was 140/88 mm Hg earlier and is now 102/64, respiratory rate is 22 breaths/minute, and pulse oximetry reading is 99% on room air. What cardiac rhythm is the patient experiencing?

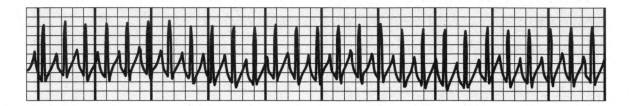

a. Junctional tachycardia

b. Sinus rhythm

c. Sinus tachycardia

d. Stable supraventricular tachycardia

25. What is the appropriate first treatment for this patient?

a. Vagal maneuvers

b. Adenosine 3 mg IV

c. Adenosine 12 mg IV

d. Normal saline 1 to 2 L bolus

26. Mr. Plankton is complaining of difficulty in breathing and feels a rapid heart rate. His cardiac monitor reads a rate of 179 bpm. What are examples of safe vagal maneuvers with consideration of Mr. Planktons age of 89?

a. Bearing down and holding his breathe

b. Rubbing hard on both eye balls or the carotid massage

c. Coughing and pushing himself up in bed

d. Both a and c

27. What signs or symptoms would lead you to believe the patient is becoming unstable?

a. Hypotension

b. Headache

c. Decrease in urine output

d. Palpitations

28. Mr. Plankton's vital signs are deteriorating due to the supraventricular tachycardia, which did not respond to vagal maneuvers. The heart rate is up to 200/minute. The patient's blood pressure is 110/48 mm Hg. The pulse oximetry reading is 96%. He has a patent IV in his upper arm. What is the next recommended intervention?

a. Synchronized cardioversion at 360 J

b. Synchronized cardioversion at 50 to 100 J

c. Amiodarone 300 mg IV push

d. Adenosine 6 mg IV push

29. You are evaluating a newly admitted patient to the critical care unit. Mr. Patrick Starr, a 48-year-old man with crushing chest pain - with a pain score of 10 out of 10. The patient is pale, diaphoretic, and is losing consciousness. The blood pressure is 74/32 mm Hg, the heart rate is 186/minute, the respiratory rate is 12 breaths/minute, and his peripheral pulses are very weak. The ECG displays a regular wide-complex tachycardia. What is the action you and the team should perform next?

a. Troponin levels

b. Central line need for sedation purposes

c. Amiodarone 300 mg IV

d. Immediate synchronized cardioversion

30. When an unconscious victim has tachycardia with a wide-complex, what is your first assessment?

a. Patients blood glucose and A1C level

b. Check to see if there are pulses present

c. PTT and INR results

d. Magnesium level

31. Which rhythm requires sedation and synchronized cardioversion?

a. Junctional rhythm

b. Asystole and pulseless electrical activity (PEA)

c. Sinus bradycardia

d. Unstable supraventricular tachycardia (SVT) or unstable ventricular tachycardia (VT)

32. For narrow-complex tachycardia (SVT) the drug of choice is adenosine. What is the appropriate dosing according to the latest recommendations?

a. 6 mg, then 12 mg IV push - fast and flush

b. 3 mg, then 6 mg IV push slowly

c. 6 mg, then 6 mg, then12 mg IV push - fast and flush

d. Atropine is the drug of choice at 0.5 mg IVP

33. The Rapid Response Team arrives to Mrs. Krab's bedside on a monitored unit. This 59-year-old woman is complaining of chest pressure, radiating up to her jaw. The blood pressure is 100/58 mm Hg. Her heart rate is 62 beats per minute and the respiratory rate is 16 breaths/minute. Pulse oximetry reading is 99%. Which assessment is most important at this time?

a. Arterial blood gas

b. Blood glucose

c. Obtaining a 12-lead ECG

d. Chest X-Ray

34. You are at your high school reunion. You see a crowd gather and you hear a commotion. You assist in the rescue and assess the victim who is unresponsive, not breathing and there is no pulse. Someone else is calling 911 and is activating the emergency response system. What is your next action?

a. Open the airway and deliver 2 quick breaths

b. Start chest compression with a rate of at 100 to 120/minute

c. Wait for the catering hall to locate an AED

d. Turn the victim on his/her side to the rescue position

35. You have turned on the AED, and the pads are applied. The AED is not analyzing the rhythm as expected. What should you and the team do?

a. Assume there is a pulse and get the victim a drink of water

b. Assume there is a pulse and place the victim in the recovery position

c. Leave and call 911

d. Go back to chest compressions immediately

36. During cardiac arrest, IV bolus of medications and fluids are to be administered. Which IV access site is usually used in the hospitalized patient at the time of arrest for medication administration?

a. A peripheral or antecubital line

b. Endotracheal tube is the best access if available

c. A femoral central line

d. An intraosseous access

37. As an ACLS provider and member of the medical team providing care for a victim in cardiac arrest, you are expected to:

a. Be proficient in skills according to your licensure and scope of practice

b. Provide all emergency treatments needed

c. Be the team leader if you are the loudest one at the scene

d. Follow all directions, without discussing other or better treatment modalities

38. Before the victim is intubated, which is the proper ventilation rate in a respiratory arrest victim?

a. Deliver one breath every 30 compressions

b. Deliver breaths every 10 to 15 seconds

c. Deliver one breath every 5 to 6 seconds (10 to 12 breaths per minute)

d. Deliver two breaths every 30 seconds

39. You are assisting in a traumatic resuscitation. The patient is intubated and CPR is continuous. After 2 minutes of CPR (5 cycles), the team leader requests a pulse check. The ECG monitor displays the rhythm below, and the patient has no pulse. You resume the chest compressions, and an IV is in place. What is the next recommendation?

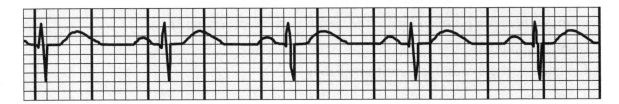

a. Administer an amiodarone infusion

b. Administer 1 mg of epinephrine

c. Initiate hypothermia protocol

d. Give 1 mg of atropine

40. A patient is brought into the emergency department with signs and symptoms of a stroke. A non-contrast CAT Scan was done and no signs of hemorrhage is seen by the radiologist. What treatment must be considered immediately?

a. Repeating the CAT Scan in 24 hours

b. Preparing for a cranial burr hole

c. Administering 2 mg of epinephrine

d. Starting the fibrinolytic tPa as soon as possible

41. What would be considered an error during a resuscitation effort?

a. PETCO2 greater than 10 mm Hg

b. Not giving ventilations immediately

c. Having the family present in the room

d. Stopping compressions for more than 10 seconds

42. What can you do to ensure adequate compressions?

a. Compress 1-1/2 to 2 inches

b. Compressions to ventilation ratio of 15:2

c. Lift hands up enough for adequate chest recoil with each compression

d. Ventilate as fast as possible

43. The practitioner wants you to charge the paddles. Why would you recommend the use of the pads in the defibrillation of ventricular fibrillation?

a. The paddles do not work anymore

b. The pads allow for a quicker and more efficient defibrillation

c. The pads deliver less joules than the paddles

d. There is no advantage to the pads, everyone still likes to use paddles

44. Which of the following has the best description for Pulseless Electrical Activity (PEA) listed?

a. Asystole without a pulse is PEA

b. Torsades de pointes with a pulse is PEA

c. Sinus bradycardia without a pulse is PEA

d. Ventricular tachycardia with a pulse is PEA

45. When the patient has a confirmed advanced airway in place what is the correct way to do compressions and ventilations?

a. Provide continuous chest compressions with 1 breath every 6 seconds (10 breaths/minute)

b. Provide 4 breathes every 6 seconds during the compression pause

c. Provide compressions and breaths with a 30:2 ratio

d. Provide compressions and breaths with a 15:2 ratio

46. You are assessing a 63-year-old man brought by ambulance into the cardiac triage area. His wife dialed 911 and the EMS brought him in. The EMS brought in the patient's 12-lead ECG and gave the patient a chewable aspirin (160 to 325 mg). Nitro SL did not relieve his chest pain. The paramedics noticed STEMI (ST elevated MI) changes in the ECG. Their initial vital signs are: blood pressure is 168/92 mm Hg, the heart rate is 100 beats per minute, the respiratory rate is 14 breaths/minute, and the pulse oximetry reading is 97%. What is the next treatment and assessment you and your team should be performing?

a. Send patient for a CT scan of his brain

b. Give morphine sulfate (MSO4) 2 to 4 mg for pain and draw blood specimens

c. Give fluids and obtain if any allergy to antibiotics

d. IV nitroglycerin infusion STAT and reassess the blood pressure

47. When is the appropriate time to give Atropine 0.5 mg IV bolus/push?

a. 3rd degree heart block

b. Unstable bradycardia

c. Asystole

d. Pulseless electrical activity (PEA)

48. While treating a patient with dizziness, a blood pressure of 68/30 mm Hg, and cool, clammy skin, you see this lead II ECG rhythm. What rhythm is this and what is the treatment?

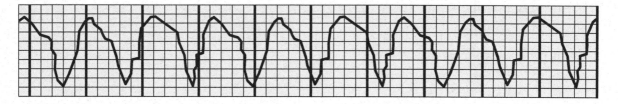

a. 1st degree heart block – no treatment necessary

b. 2nd degree heart block type II (Mobitz II) - Atropine 0.5 mg, TCP, dopamine infusion

c. Monomorphic Ventricular Tachycardia - Synchronize cardioversion and Amiodarone 150 mg IVPB over 10 minutes

d. Torsades de Pointes – Magnesium 1 to 2 Grams IV infusion

49. You are caring for a patient with pneumonia who is orally intubated and is sedated and on a ventilator. The high-pressure alarm is sounding, what is your assessment and intervention?

a. Patient is disconnected from the ventilator, hook it back together

b. Secretions accumulating; suction while pulling the catheter out; but not for more than 10 seconds

c. Tubing is kinked, wait for the respiratory therapist to check the machine

d. Suction during insertion but not more than 15 seconds, then hyperventilate

50. What is the correct dose of aspirin for the patient complaining of chest pain?

a. 1,000 mg

b. 160 to 325 mg

c. 2 enteric-coated tablets

d. 3 enteric-coated tablets

51. What is the lowest systolic blood pressure goal that guides the use of vasoactive medications and fluid boluses?

a. 90 mm Hg systolic

b. 80 mm Hg systolic

c. 70 mm Hg systolic

d. 65 mm Hg systolic

52. The team is hanging fluids for a patient post cardiac arrest to increase the blood pressure. What is the recommended initial fluid bolus?

a. 50 to 100 ml per hour

b. 5 to 10 liters of warmed dextrose fluid

c. Wait for the insertion of a right atrial catheter

d. 1 to 2 liters of isotonic or crystalloid fluid

53. Which treatments are no longer recommended during cardiac arrest?

a. Epinephrine IV push, Amiodarone

b. 1 to 2 liters of fluid and vasoconstricting medications

c. Cricoid pressure, continuous 100% oxygen, atropine, vasopressin

d. Wait for the insertion of a right atrial catheter

54. Therapeutic Hypothermia, at 32 to 36 degrees celsius, often called "Code Chill" or Temperature Management has been used to treat patients' post-cardiac arrest. The ideal candidate for hypothermia protocol is which patient?

a. A victim who is resuscitated, but won't wake up

b. A victim who remains pulseless after 25 minutes of CPR

c. A victim who is able to walk into the ED after a head injury

d. A victim of cardiac arrest who must have surgery to repair abdominal gunshots

55. The purpose of the 24-hour hypothermia protocol in the post cardiac arrest victim is . . . ?

a. Improving survival by reducing free radicals and decreasing oxygen demand

b. Increases the body metabolism and healing powers

c. Prevents a fever due to infection diseases

d. Shivering encourages the dying patient to wake up

56. After the return of spontaneous circulation (ROSC), what are the emergency priorities?

a. Stabilize the vital signs, and transport the patient to a facility that can perform a percutaneous coronary angioplasty intervention (PCI)

b. Obtaining the patient's insurance card to obtain approval for hospitalization

c. Have the family involved in the direct care of the patient

d. Administering 100% oxygen

57. You have been doing chest compressions on a victim in the cafeteria. Another employee brings over the Automatic External Defibrillator (AED). What should you tell the other rescuer?

a. Tell them to call the supervisor, that you will be late for work

b. Tell them to double check the pulse on the victim while you are doing compressions

c. Tell them to wait until you have done CPR for 10 minutes

d. Tell them to turn it on, and follow directions to apply pads

58. The Automatic External Defibrillator (AED) does not analyze the victim's rhythm once you apply the pads. What is the next action to take?

a. Reapply the pads

b. Wait for another AED to arrive, while you rest for a minute

c. Go back to fast and deep compressions

d. Use a head tilt chin lift maneuver and see if the patient started to breath on their own

59. The Emergency Medical Services (EMS) arrives on the scene of a traumatic cardiac arrest, where you have started CPR. There is an organized rhythm on the monitor but still no pulse. What are the causes of PEA?

a. Hyperglycemia

b. Metabolic Alkalosis

c. Cardiac tamponade and tension pneumothorax

d. Missing doses of calcium channel blockers

60. The Emergency Medical Services (EMS) arrives with a patient in found unconscious after falling off a ladder. The patient is pulseless and remains in pulseless electrical activity. This prolonged situation continues as CPR continues with 3 more doses of epinephrine given. The team should be discussing the possibility of . . . ?

a. Terminating efforts

b. Tension pneumothorax

c. Hypothermia protocols

d. Atropine IV push

61. A 92-year-old man is admitted to your unit. As you take his vital signs he has a loss of consciousness and you cannot feel a pulse. What needs to be done immediately?

a. Call the emergency response team and begin chest compressions

b. Have someone re-check for a pulse as soon as possible

c. Assume he has a DNR and withhold lifesaving efforts

d. Apply oxygen and see if he regains consciousness

62. Once a victim is defibrillated, what is the first drug of choice in cardiac arrest?

a. Amiodarone 300 mg IV push

b. Epinephrine 1 mg IV push

c. Sodium bicarbonate IV push

d. Magnesium 1 to 2 grams

63. Your victim collapsed at a wedding party. The team is doing compressions and you are ventilating. You are having a difficult time getting rise and fall of the chest. You ask for an oral airway. You are given a few choices. How will you select the correct size for the oral pharyngeal airway?

a. Select the largest airway available, to get the most oxygen in

b. Select the smallest airway available, so you can suction as well

c. Measure the oral airway from the corner of the mouth/lip to the angle of the jaw near the ear

d. Measure the oral airway from the center of the mouth to the angle of the jaw near the ear

64. When is a transcutaneous pacemaker recommended?

a. Refractory V-Tach or V-Fib

b. Sinus Bradycardia

c. Unstable 3rd degree heart block

d. Supraventricular Tachycardia

65. Vagal maneuvers have not been effective for this patient in supraventricular tachycardia (SVT). The patient's blood pressure is stable. What is the dosing of adenosine for supraventricular tachycardia (SVT)?

a. 6 mg then 12 mg IV over 12 minutes

b. 6 mg then 12 mg IV push fast, and flush

c. 150 mg in 100 ml over 10 minutes

d. Adenosine is not recommended in SVT

66. Supraventricular tachycardia is caused by . . . ?

a. Fever and dehydration

b. Sick sinus syndrome

c. Anxiety

d. Reentry or re-excitation of an impulse

67. If both the vagal maneuvers and adenosine is ineffective in resolving the patient's supraventricular tachycardia (SVT), the blood pressure is dropping, and the level of consciousness is changing, what is the next treatment of choice?

a. Synchronized cardioversion at 50 to 100 joules

b. Synchronized cardioversion at 360 joules

c. Unsynchronized cardioversion at 360 joules

d. Cardioversion should always be avoided in tachycardia arrhythmias

68. You are performing high quality CPR on an adult victim of cardiac arrest. Describe the compressions.

a. At two (2) to two-and-one-half (2-1/2) inches deep, at least 100 to 120 compressions per minute

b. Use two hands, pressing on the lower half of the sternum

c. Giving 15 compressions to 2 breaths

d. Both a and b

69. At what points can the rescuer check a pulse on unconscious victims?

a. Check the pulse initially after calling the emergency services

b. Check the pulse at random intervals during the code

c. Check the pulse at the 5 cycle two-minute compressor switch intervals

d. Both a and c

70. Mrs. Cheeks is experiencing dizziness and weakness. Her cardiac monitor has a regular rhythm with a heart rate of 41. Her blood pressure had been 106/50, RR of 12, O2 saturation of 95%. You retake the blood pressure and it is 90/44. You see this rhythm on the monitor. What rhythm is displayed?

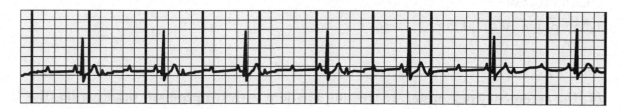

a. 2nd degree Type II (Mobitz II)

b. Third degree heart block- complete heart block

c. Junctional rhythm

d. Sinus bradycardia

71. What is the initial treatment to increase Mrs. Cheek's heart rate, and restore stability?

a. Atropine 1 mg IV push

b. Atropine 0.5 mg IV push

c. Epinephrine 1 mg IV push

d. Epinephrine 0.5 mg IV push

72. Initial treatments are not effective in increasing Mrs. Cheek's bradycardia. What are subsequent treatments to increase the patient's heart rate?

a. Atropine 1 mg IV push and a dobutamine infusion

b. Epinephrine 1 mg IV push and a vasopressin infusion

c. Transcutaneous pacemaker and a dopamine infusion

d. Adenosine 6 mg IV push and a Cardizem infusion

73. Which is a standard treatment procedure for patients with STEMI (ST elevated MI)?

a. Reperfusion therapy within 90 minutes

b. Epinephrine IVP

c. Defibrillation

d. Morphine 10 to 20 mg

74. The emergency personnel are treating a patient with symptomatic bradycardia. The team-leader asks for Atropine 1 mg IVP, and repeat every 3 to 5 minutes. You know the recommended dose is 0.5 mg every 3 to 5 minutes, with the maximum of 3 mg. You speak up in a professional manner to recommend the dose of 0.5 mg of Atropine, as in the 2015 ACLS guidelines. What is this behavior in team dynamics called?

a. Mutual Respect

b. Constructive Intervention

c. Clear Messages

d. Closed Loop Communication

75. An Ischemic stroke is . . . ?

a. The most common stroke, caused by a clot

b. The most common stroke, caused by a hemorrhage

c. Very uncommon, caused by exposure to heat

d. Very uncommon stroke, caused by exposure to prolonged cold temperatures.

76. The emergency services will respond to a stroke victim and perform a stroke assessment on the victim. Which of the following is not one of the 3 assessments/tests the EMS uses to identify stroke?

a. Slurred speech

b. Arm drift

c. Facial droop

d. Increase in hunger

77. What disorder can mimic the signs and symptoms of stroke?

a. Appendicitis

b. Hypoglycemia

c. Pneumonia

d. Increase in hunger

78. A routine test for patients who have had a stroke before they take any oral medications or liquids is . . . ?

a. Sweat Test

b. Dysphagia and swallow screening

c. Sobriety Test

d. Chvostek Sign

79. The nasopharyngeal airway . . . ?

a. Is used to deliver medications when there is no IV access

b. Is measured from the tip of the nose to the corner of the mandible

c. Provides a passageway for air between the nose and the pharynx

d. Both b and c

80. What is the immediate and priority test required in the Emergency Department or Stroke Center for patients with signs and symptoms of a stroke?

a. Full body MRI

b. Non-contrast CAT scan of the brain

c. The test is not priority until the symptoms subside

d. An exercise stress echocardiogram

81. The team began ventilations on a patient with respiratory distress. The ventilations delivered has improved the oxygenation, however the carbon dioxide level on the capnography monitor is 28. What direction would you give to the ventilator?

a. Speed up the ventilations to reduce the CO2 please

b. Slow down the ventilations to 10 to 12 bpm, to prevent hyperoxia, and reduction of cardiac output

c. Slow down the ventilations till the oxygen level is below 90 mm Hg

d. Initiate a sodium bicarbonate infusion

82. Mr. Jenkins, a 67-year-old man, is brought into the ED. He has vague complaints of chest and arm pain. He had been nauseous earlier. The Emergency staff explains he may be having a heart attack. He is on a cardiac monitor, and has a peripheral IV. He is receiving oxygen and a pulse oximeter is attached. B/P is stable. What is the next priority?

a. Continuous waveform capnography

b. 12-lead ECG

c. Isuprel infusion

d. Lidocaine infusion

83. Mr. Neptune has premature ventricular contractions and short runs of ventricular tachycardia. What is the recommended medication to reduce the ventricular irritability?

a. Lidocaine 100 mg

b. Aspirin 160 to 325 mg

c. Amiodarone 150 mg over 10 minutes

d. Epinephrine infusion

84. Mr. Neptune is experiencing ventricular tachycardia. He is losing consciousness but has a pulse. What is the recommendation for cardioversion for this patient?

a. 360 unsynchronized joules

b. 360 synchronized joules

c. 100 unsynchronized joules

d. 100 synchronized joules

85. To prepare for emergencies, what would be the correct steps for operating an AED?

a. Attach electrode pads, turn on the AED, shock the patient, analyze the rhythm

b. Turn on the AED, apply pads, analyze the rhythm, clear the patient, deliver shock

c. Attach electrode pads, check pulse, shock patient, analyze rhythm

d. Check pulse, attach electrode pads, analyze rhythm, shock patient

86. Mrs. Puff, an 85-year-old woman, is being evaluated for dizziness from a slow heart rate. You are measuring the PR interval on her ECG strip. Normally this interval is 0.12 to 0.20 seconds (3 to 5 small boxes). Her consistent but wide PR interval measures 11 little squares x .04 seconds = 0.44 seconds. What rhythm is she in?

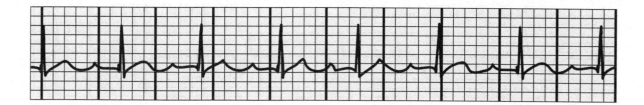

a. Junctional rhythm

b. 1st degree AV block

c. 2nd degree AV block, type I, Mobitz I (Wenckebach)

d. 3rd degree heart block

87. Mrs. Puff is still stable, but her heart rate decreases to 40 bpm. You notice an irregular rhythm and you re-measure the PR interval on her ECG strip. You notice the PR interval is getting longer and longer then drops a QRS. There are groupings of QRS's and then a P-wave without the QRS. What rhythm is she in now?

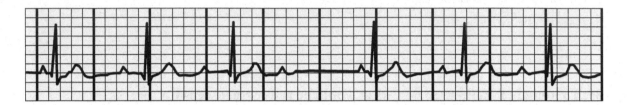

a. Junctional rhythm

b. 1st degree AV block

c. 2nd degree AV block, type I, Mobitz I (Wenckebach)

d. 3rd degree heart block

88. Miss Karin is a patient in the cardiac care unit. In evaluating her ECG rhythm you notice a heart block, because there are more P-wave than QRS waves. You notice that there isn't any relationship between the P-waves and the QRS waves. What rhythm is Miss Karin experiencing?

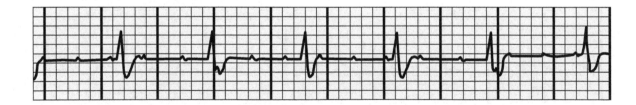

a. 3rd degree heart block

b. 2nd degree AV block, type I, Mobitz I (Wenckebach)

c. 1st degree AV block

d. Junctional rhythm

89. Mr. Hazelton is a patient in the cardiac care unit. In evaluating his ECG rhythm you notice a slowing of the heart rate to 47 bpm. The rhythm is regular with narrow QRS's. You do not see any P-waves. What rhythm is Mr. Hazelton experiencing?

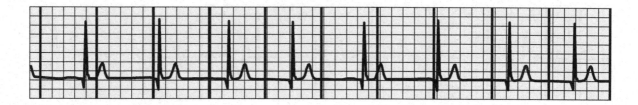

a. Junctional rhythm

b. 1st degree AV block

c. 2nd degree AV block, type I, Mobitz I (Wenckebach)

d. 3rd degree heart block

90. In reviewing the heart blocks, you know that a 2nd degree type II (Mobitz II) heart block consists of . . . ?

a. More P than Q waves

b. Narrow or wide QRS's

c. Every time there is a QRS wave, it is "married" to the P-wave and the PR intervals are consistent when they exist

d. All of the above

91. You are with the Rapid Response Team, and are called to the room of Mr. Simon, a 55-year-old male patient. He is awake but complaining of severe dizziness. His blood pressure is 94/40. Atropine has not worked. What is the next treatment of choice?

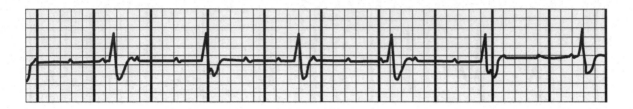

a. Magnesium 1 to 2grams

b. Hemodialysis

c. Transcutaneous pacemaker

d. Precordial thump

92. Mr. Simon needs immediate treatment for the hypotension caused by the above rhythm. What are the first considerations?

a. Amiodarone and Synchronized Cardioversion

b. Pacemaker and a dopamine or epinephrine infusion

b. Immediate fluid resuscitation

d. Adenosine and Synchronized Cardioversion

93. What is the correct dosing of Amiodarone in treating Ventricular Tachycardia with a pulse present?

a. Amiodarone 6 mg IV push

b. Amiodarone 300 mg IV push

c. Amiodarone 150 mg in 100 ml over 10 minutes

d. Give Atropine 0.5 mg IV push instead

94. When the patient becomes unstable with a wide-complex tachycardia, what is the next treatment of choice?

a. Amiodarone 300 mg IV push

b. Amiodarone 150 mg in 100 ml over 10 minutes

c. Synchronized Cardioversion at 100 joules

d. Unsynchronized Cardioversion at 200 joules

95. You are at a soccer game and the crowd is pushing and shoving. When the crowd disperses there is an unconscious victim near a fence. He is not breathing. What is your next action?

a. Call for assistance and check the victims pulse

b. Ensure that yourself and other rescuers are safe

c. Leave the scene as not to be accused of harming the victim

d. Both a and b

96. You are caring for a patient who has been admitted to the hospital for rapid atrial fibrillation. The cardiologist has tried to treat the patient with calcium channel blockers. But the fast heart rate is now causing the blood pressure to drop as well. The team is preparing to sedate and synchronize cardiovert. How many joules will the cardiologist request?

a. 50 to 100 joules

b. 120 to 200 joules

c. 200 to 360 joules

d. Unsynchronized 360 joules

97. You are caring for the patient pre-procedure. He complains of feeling his heart racing. Vital signs are B/P 112/64, HR 168, RR 12, pulse oximetry 95%. His lungs are clear and the 12-lead ECG has been repeated. What are the best options for the team are in providing care for this patient?

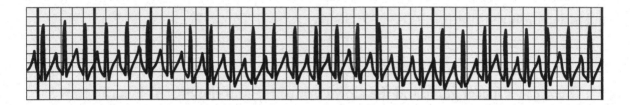

a. Look at the ECG to determine if the QRS's are narrow or wide

b. Consider cardioversion if the patient becomes unstable

c. Consider vagal maneuvers, adenosine, and contact a cardiologist

d. All of the above

98. The team has the pads on the cardiac arrest victim's chest, the defibrillator is charging, chest compressions continue until the team leader ensures patient and team safety by stating I'm going to shock on three. One, two, three, everyone clear. What happens after the shock is delivered?

a. The bed sheets are changed

b. The team returns to doing compressions

c. The team checks the pulses

d. The team will deliver 2 more consecutive defibrillations

99. You are assigned to care for Mr. Pabst, a patient in the Emergency Department. He is drowsy, but easy to arouse, and appears intoxicated. His history reveals alcoholism, hypertension, and an old ECG on file shows prolonged Q-T intervals. The cardiac monitor alarm alerts you to an arrhythmia. What is the rhythm below?

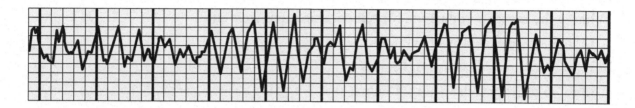

a. Torsade de Pointes (Polymorphic V-Tach)

b. Monomorphic V-Tach

c. Commotio cordis

d. Atrial flutter

100. Mr. Star's vital signs remain stable despite the continuing dysrhythmia present on the cardiac monitor. The emergency department team is preparing for cardioversion and applies the pads to his chest. In the meantime, as the team leader, what treatment would you want for this patient?

a. Adenosine 6 then 12 mg IV push

b. Magnesium 1 to 2 grams, IV fast infusion

c. Dobutamine infusion

d. Dopamine infusion

101. Ms. Pearl is brought into the emergency department by the EMS. She had pulled her car over to the side of the road, and she slumped over and went ito cardiac arrest. EMS was called and bystanders intitiated effective chest compressions. The paramedics arrived and defibrillated Mrs. Pearl back into a sinus rhythm. The team is now discussing the initiation of the hyperthermia temperature management protocol. What is the recommendations for temperature management?

a. 32 to 36 degrees Celsius for 2 hours

b. 32 to 36 degrees Celsius for 4 hours

c. 32 to 36 degrees Celsius for 24 hours

d. 28 to 32 degrees Celsius for 48 hours

Part 3:
The Answers
and
Explanations

Notes

Answers And Explanations For The ACLS Questions

1. When a victim has and advanced airway inserted (intubated) what is the recommended method for performing high-quality CPR?

d. Continuous chest compressions with 10 ventilations per minute. This is the recommendation for ventilation in all age groups of victims with advanced airways. Initially, we usually hyperventilate for 15 to 30 seconds to reverse respiratory acidosis, but we must slow down to prevent respiratory alkalosis, to the rate of one breath every 6 to 8 seconds.

2. While you are taking your patient's blood pressure, the patient gasps and loses consciousness. After calling for help and determining that the patient is not breathing, you cannot palpate the pulse within 10 seconds. What is your next action?

a. Begin chest compressions. Any doubt of breathing or pulse the rescuer must begin chest compressions with in 10 seconds. Gasps (or agonal breathing) is not effective breathing. There should be continuous chest compressions without interruptions longer than 10 seconds.

3. What is the advantage of using quantitative waveform capnography during cardiac arrest?

c. Allows for monitoring of CPR quality and measures expired carbon dioxide. Continuous waveform capnography allows for monitoring of CPR quality and measures expired carbon dioxide. If the PETCO2 is less than 10, then the rescuer must compress harder. The monitoring of CO_2 also indicates that the endotracheal tube is probably placed appropriately until a confirmatory x-ray is taken.

4. The Emergency Department (ED) team is attempting to resuscitate a victim who was brought into the ED in Ventricular Fibrillation (V-Fib) with CPR in progress. The ED staff delivered 4 shocks, 3 doses of epinephrine, amiodarone 300 mg, 2 liters of normal saline, and the victim converted to asystole, which persists despite and high-quality CPR. What is your next consideration?

a. Discuss with the team, terminating the resuscitative efforts. When the victim was in V-Fib there was a good chance of survival. Now that the victim is in sustained asystole the team should consider the reversible causes of cardiac arrest and then termination of efforts. The 2015 guidelines do not recommend vasopressin for victims of cardiac arrest.

5. The team is treating a cardiac arrest victim. The patient is intubated, a peripheral antecubital IV is inserted and continuous chest compressions are performed. Minutes later you reassess the waveform on the capnography screen and a PETCO2 level of 6 mm Hg is displayed. What does a PETCO2 of less than 10 mm Hg signify to the team?

c. Chest compressions may not be effective. If the PETCO2 is less that 10 mm Hg, the compressor must be encouraged by the team to do deeper compressions.

6. Prior to delivering a defibrillation (shock) to a patient you must first . . . ?

c. Be sure "oxygen flow is clear" from patient's chest. Risks of sparks are minimal using the defibrillator pads, but oxygen flowing increases the risk of fire if there is any sparks. Pulse checks are not recommended if it will delay the continuation of chest compressions.

7. What is the depth of compressions for adults in cardiac arrest?

b. 2 to 2-1/2 inches. Two (2) to two-and-a-half (2-1/2) inches is the correct depth of compressions for adults requiring CPR. The ratio is 30 compressions to 2 breaths (30:2) in adult CPR.

8. How can the team minimize any interruptions during CPR to less than 10 seconds?

c. Continue CPR while charging the defibrillator, and resume immediately after the shock. This is the most efficient way to reduce delays and get immediately back to the chest compressions.

9. What action besides starting chest compressions is extremely important in the Basic Life Support Survey?

b. Early defibrillation with an AED. Early defibrillation offers the only chance for survival for a victim in a shockable rhythm. Getting blood sugar results, hypothermia protocol and medicated infusions is initiated after resuscitation occurs.

10. The team is continuing resuscitation efforts in the doctor's office. After a shock of 200 J the patient remains in ventricular fibrillation. CPR is continued for two minutes, epinephrine 1 mg IV push given. What is the next treatment recommended?

b. Defibrillation at 360 J. Maximum joules available is recommended in the V-Fib algorithm, if the initial shock did not work. Amiodarone will be the next drug of choice, at the dose of 300 mg IVP. Sotalol (100 mg) and Procainamide are not first line medications.

11. When using continuous capnography, what evidence is a sign of ineffective chest compressions?

c. PETCO2 < 10 mm Hg. Compressions need to be deep enough to achieve a PETCO2 greater than 10 mm Hg. Pupil response is not a reliable sign of perfusion. Urine output is based on many factors, and is not a verification of effective CPR and cardiac output.

12. What is the recommended maximum time period for pausing in chest compressions?

b. Ten (10) seconds or less. There is a ten (10) second or less rule for best outcomes. Begin chest compressions within 10 seconds of finding a pulseless victim, and do not pause compressions for more than 10 seconds.

13. Why is the rapid response team (RRT) summoned to the patient's room?

c. To assist the existing team in identifying the problem and preventing further deterioration. The Rapid Response Team (RRT) is an assigned team that responds to a call, in the hospital, when there is a change in the patient's condition, where this team can assist to identify the problem, treat appropriately and prevent cardiac arrest.

14. Which of the following actions is done first to restore circulation, oxygenation and ventilation to unresponsive pulseless victims?

d. High-quality CPR. The priority in a pulseless victim is to provide high-quality CPR. Procedures, ECG, X-Rays and ABG's are done after a pulse returns and the victim is stabilized.

15. Which of the following will enhance the quality of chest compressions during cardiac arrest situations?

c. Switch providers about every 2 minutes or every 5 cycles. To provide continuous high quality CPR the rescuers need to switch roles about every 2 minutes or every 5 cycles. This would prevent exhaustion as well. Compressions are done on the lower one-half of the sternum at the rate of 100 to 120 compressions per minute.

16. You are caring for an adult victim in respiratory failure. The patient is attempting to breath independently. There is a strong pulse but you must assist with ventilations. What is the recommended rate of assisting ventilations with a bag-valve-mask device for this patient?

a. 1 breath every 5 to 6 seconds. This is the rate for breaths for someone who has a pulse but is having trouble breathing on their own. Two breaths are given during CPR (30:2).

17. You are receiving a patient into the Emergency Department who has positive signs and symptoms of a stroke. You realize this diagnosis is disabling and has a high risk of mortality. What is the initial plan for this patient when they arrive to the ED?

a. The patient needs a non-contrast CAT scan within 25 minutes of arrival. For a victim with signs and symptoms of stroke, it should be read within 45 minutes. Diagnosing an ischemic or hemorrhagic stroke will help the team correctly treat the patient. The patient's blood pressure must be within the guidelines prior to treating with the fibrinolytic rtPA, if an ischemic stroke is diagnosed. Blood pressure is acceptable when lowered to 170/90, but not to a "normal B/P", for the brain tissue is used to high perfusion pressures.

18. A paramedic is evaluating a 67-year-old man. Upon interview of the patient they recognize slurred and slowing of the man's speech. The blood pressure of 180/98 mm Hg, a heart rate of 96/minute, a non-labored respiratory rate of 20 breaths/minute, and a pulse oximetry reading of 98%. The ECG displays sinus rhythm. What action would be performed next?

b. A Pre-hospital Stroke Scale, and notify the ED. The EMS responders will perform a the Cincinnatti Stroke Scale, which tests for facial droop, arm drift, and slurred speech. Patients with one of these 3 findings have a 72% probability of acute stroke. Fibrinolytic therapy rtPA cannot be given until a CAT scan is done, to rule out a hemorrhagic stroke. The EMS will notify the emergency department, their estimated time of arrival, so the CAT Scan is made available.

19. Prior to the arrival of the stroke patient to the ED, the Radiology Department calls you with the news that the CAT scanner is not working temporarily, and that repairs are being made. What should you do in this situation?

b. Ensure a safe disposition and divert the ambulance to a nearby hospital if possible. The patient needs a CAT SCAN to diagnose the stroke, and cannot wait for lengthy repairs. MRI is an excellent alternative test, but it takes much longer.

20. You arrive in minutes to a Rapid Response Team call for a patient who has a change in mental status and right arm weakness. The team initially obtained a blood pressure of 188/110 mm Hg, the pulse rate is 90/minute, the respiratory rate is 14 breaths/minute, and the pulse oximetry reading is 93% on room air. The lead II ECG displays sinus rhythm. The blood glucose level is within normal limits. What intervention should be done next?

d. Head CT scan. With an elevated blood pressure and change in mental status a non-contrast CT scan of the head to rule out stroke or neurological problems is a priority. Blood glucose levels may be evaluated with changes in mental status. The patient may need oxygen, but 100% is excessive.

21. You are participating in a rescue mission. The death toll is rising. Your team is searching the area for survivors. When finding victims when would it be inappropriate to initiate or continue chest compressions?

a. There are signs of rigor mortis and post-mortem lividity. If there are signs of rigor mortis and post-mortem lividity, the victim has been dead for a prolonged period of time. Beginning CPR would be futile. The rescue team will triage the victims and make decisions on the priority of patients.

22. Your 68-year-old patient, Mrs. Sandy Cheeks, who has emphysema, is in the telemetry unit. She is complaining of dizziness and fatigue. The patient's heart rate is 40 bpm, the blood pressure is 96/54 mm Hg, and the respiratory rate is 18 breaths/minute. The oxygen saturation remains unchanged at 94%. What is the appropriate first medication?

c. A focused assessment, 12-lead ECG, and consider Atropine 0.5 mg. Atropine 0.5 mg is given for unstable bradycardia, every 3 to 5 minutes with the maximum of 3 mg. Epinephrine 1 mg is used in V-fib, Asystole, and PEA. Adenosine 6 mg, then 12 mg is used for rapid rates in SVT.

23. Mrs. Cheek's initial atropine doses were ineffective, and the physician requests a vasoactive infusion. Her blood pressure is now 84/50. She is responding to your commands, and is OK with laying flat in her bed. What is an appropriate medicated infusion for this patient?

a. Dopamine 2 to 10 mcg/kg per minute. Lowest dose dopamine may dilate the coronary arteries and help the heart pump. Titration to a higher dose may be necessary. The correct dosing for epinephrine infusion in symptomatic bradycardia, if needed is 0.1 to 0.5 mcg/kg/minute. Consider a pacemaker (transcutaneous or transvenous) whenever available.

24. Mr. Sheldon J. Plankton, age 89, rings his call bell and complains of palpitations. The patient's heart rate is 172 minute, blood pressure was 140/88 mm Hg earlier and is now 102/64, respiratory rate is 22 breaths/minute, and pulse oximetry reading is 99% on room air. What cardiac rhythm is the patient experiencing?

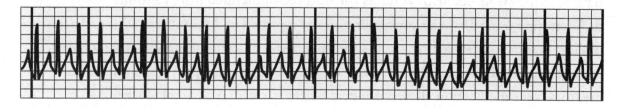

d. Stable supraventricular tachycardia. The heart rate is over 150 bpm, with a B/P within normal limits.

25. What is the appropriate first treatment for this patient?

a. Vagal maneuvers. Coughing and bearing down are vagal maneuvers that may convert the rythm. If the patient does not respond, Adenosine 6 mg, then 12 mg, and synchronized cardioversion will be considered.

26. Mr. Plankton is complaining of difficulty in breathing and feels a rapid heart rate. His cardiac monitor reads a rate of 179 bpm. What are examples of safe vagal maneuvers with consideration of Mr. Plankton's age of 89?

d. Both a and c. Bearing down and holding his breath or coughing and pushing himself up in bed are safe options for Mr. Plankton. Rubbing the eyeballs can damage recent surgical procedures, and the carotid massage is dangerous because it can dislodge plaque in the carotid artery and cause a stroke.

27. What signs or symptoms would lead you to believe the patient is becoming unstable?

a. Hypotension. Other symptoms of an unstable patient include chest pain, shortness of breath, change in mental status, and crackles in his lungs. Palpitations is uncomfortable, but not necessarily a sign of being unstable.

28. Mr. Plankton's vital signs are deteriorating due to the supraventricular tachycardia, which did not respond to vagal maneuvers. The heart rate is up to 200/minute. The patient's blood pressure is 110/48 mm Hg. The pulse oximetry reading is 96%. He has a patent IV in his upper arm. What is the next recommended intervention?

d. Adenosine 6 mg IV push. Adenosine can be repeated in 2 minutes at 12 mg. Adenosine is short acting and fast acting, so it is the preferred medication for SVT. It does have dramatic effects for 6 seconds – flat line on the monitor, chest pain and shortness of breath. Other medication choices are beta blockers, calcium channel blockers, and amiodarone.

29. You are evaluating a newly admitted patient to the critical care unit. Mr. Patrick Starr, a 48-year-old man with crushing chest pain - with a score of 10 out of 10. The patient is pale, diaphoretic, and is losing consciousness. The blood pressure is 74/32 mm Hg, the heart rate is 186/minute, the respiratory rate is 12 breaths/minute, and his peripheral pulses are very weak. The ECG displays a regular wide-complex tachycardia. What is the action you and the team should perform next?

d. Immediate synchronized cardioversion. This patient is in an unstable SVT. The blood pressure is low, and he has wide QRS's, chest pain, and has signs of deterioration and shock. Synchronized cardioversion is needed urgently. He is losing consciousness and it will be unsafe to sedate.

30. When an unconscious victim has tachycardia with a wide-complex, what is your first assessment?

b. Check to see if there are pulses present. Check pulses when an unconscious patient has any tachycardia, especially a wide QRS complex. A rapid wide QRS complex could be ventricular tachycardia (with or without a pulse).

31. Which rhythm requires sedation and synchronized cardioversion?

d. Unstable supraventricular tachycardia (SVT) or unstable ventricular tachycardia (VT). These rhythms (with a pulse) requires a synchronized cardioversion starting with 50 to 100 joules. Whenever possible, based on their blood pressure, sedation prior to a cardioversion is beneficial for the patient. If the patient was in Atrial Fibrillation 120 to 200 joules is recommended.

32. For narrow-complex tachycardia (SVT) the drug of choice is adenosine. What is the appropriate dosing according to the latest recommendations?

a. 6 mg, then 12 mg IV push - fast and flush. This is the 2015 guidelines for adenosine (3 doses are not recommended).

33. The Rapid Response Team arrives to Mrs. Krab's bedside on a monitored unit. This 59-year-old woman is complaining of chest pressure, radiating up to her jaw. The blood pressure is 100/58 mm Hg. Her heart rate is 62 beats per minute and the respiratory rate is 16 breaths/minute. Pulse oximetry reading is 99%. Which assessment is most important at this time?

c. Obtaining a 12-lead ECG. While she is still stable, an 12-lead ECG is a priority for chest pain. The diagnosis and subsequent treatments of a myocardial infarction is based on the ECG results. "MONA-B"- morphine, oxygen, nitroglycerine, aspirin (160 to 325 mg) and beta blockers are also recommendations.

34. You are at your high school reunion. You see a crowd gather and you hear a commotion. You assist in the rescue and assess the victim who is unresponsive, not breathing and there is no pulse. Someone else is calling 911 and is activating the emergency response system. What is your next action?

b. Start chest compression with a rate of at 100 to 120/minute. The priority for a pulseless victim is to start chest compressions. Healthcare professionals learn to perform 30 compressions to 2 breaths. Lay rescuers at the reunion may have learned chest compressions only. The defibrillator/AED is applied immediately and the shock is delivered after every 2 minutes of chest compressions.

35. You have turned on the AED, and the pads are applied. The AED is not analyzing the rhythm as expected. What should you and the team do?

d. Go back to chest compressions immediately. The rescuer should NEVER let more than 10 seconds go by without doing chest compressions. If the AED is not analyzing or functioning properly, go back to chest compressions IMMEDIATELY.

36. During cardiac arrest, IV bolus of medications and fluids are to be administered. Which IV access site is usually used in the hospitalized patient at the time of arrest for medication administration?

a. A peripheral or antecubital line. These are the most common initial routes for emergency miedications. If peripheral access is impossible the team may decide on a central line or intraosseous needle for access.

37. As an ACLS provider and member of the medical team providing care for a victim in cardiac arrest, you are expected to:

a. Be proficient in skills according to your licensure and scope of practice. During an emergency you may be asked to perform a skill that is not in your scope of practice (e.g. ABG's, IO insertion, intubation, cardioversion). Make it clear that you can only assist in procedures that you are credentialed in, to perform independently.

38. Before the victim is intubated, which is the proper ventilation rate in a respiratory arrest victim?

c. Deliver one breath every 5 to 6 seconds (10 to 12 breaths per minute). Once intubated, and delivering 100% oxygen, slow the rate down to one breath every 6 to 8 seconds (8 to 10 breaths per minute).

39. You are assisting in a traumatic resuscitation. The patient is intubated and CPR is continuous. After 2 minutes of CPR (5 cycles), the team leader requests a pulse check. The ECG monitor displays the rhythm below, and the patient has no pulse. You resume the chest compressions, and an IV is in place. What is the next recommendation?

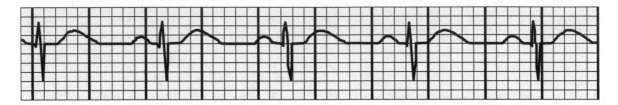

b. Administer 1 mg of epinephrine. The rhythm is pulseless electrical activity (PEA). There is a rhythm without a pulse. The 2015 guidelines recommend epinephrine 1 mg every 3 to 5 minutes no maximum. Continue CPR and consider all the reversible causes of death (the H's and T's). Vasopressin is not recommended in the 2015 guidelines. Attempt to treat the underlying cause of cardiac arrest. If the peripheral line is adequate – use it. The team can place an intraosseous needle if IV access is not available.

40. A patient is brought into the emergency department with signs and symptoms of a stroke. A non-contrast CAT Scan was done and no signs of hemorrhage is seen by the radiologist. What treatment must be considered immediately?
d. Starting the fibrinolytic tPa as soon as possible. Do this as long as there are no contraindications to the medication. A consent is usually obtained from patient/SO.

41. What would be considered an error during a resuscitation effort?
d. Stopping compressions for more than 10 seconds. Stopping compressions can result in patient deterioration. Having the family members in the room can be distracting, but it is allowed. Ventilations are important, but getting to the compressions is the priority. Even switching compressors should be completed in less than 5 seconds to avoid any delays in compressions. PETCO2 greater than 10 mm Hg would mean compressions are effective.

42. What can you do to ensure adequate compressions?

c. Lift hands up enough for adequate chest recoil with each compression. This allows for cardiac refill and high quality chest compressions. Compressions for adults are at 2 to 2-1/2 inches deep, at 30:2 or continuous compressions if there is an advanced airway.

43. The practitioner wants you to charge the paddles. Why would you recommend the use of the pads in the defibrillation of ventricular fibrillation?

b. The pads allow for a quicker and more efficient defibrillation. When using pads there is no need to use jelly or saline gauze. The pads are ready to use, and adhere well to the skin when smeared down evenly. Hair on the chest may interfere with the pads adhering properly. Pads are not universal so make sure they are a correct fit for your unit's defibrillator/AED. Pads are made for the transcutaneous pacemakers (TCP) as well, or as pacer-defib combo pads.

44. Which of the following has the best description for Pulseless Electrical Activity (PEA) listed?

c. Sinus bradycardia without a pulse is PEA. Any rhythm without a pulse is PEA. Often this rhythm will deteriorate by slowing down and then convert to asystole if CPR and other treatments are not initiated. Epinephrine, every 3 to 5 minutes, and treat the underlying cause of cardiac arrest (the H's and T's) is recommended. Treat hypoxia, hypovolemia, hydrogen ions (acidosis), hyper or hypokalemia, tension pneumothorax, cardiac tamponade, toxins (drug overdose), trauma, cardiac and pulmonary thrombosis.

45. When the patient has a confirmed advanced airway in place what is the correct way to do compressions and ventilations?

a. Provide continuous chest compressions with 1 breath every 6 seconds (10 breaths/minute). Slowing the ventilation rate down will prevent oxygen toxicity which causes reduced cardiac output.

46. You are assessing a 63-year-old man brought by ambulance into the cardiac triage area. His wife dialed 911 and the EMS brought him in. The EMS brought in the patient's 12-lead ECG and gave the patient a chewable aspirin (160 to 325 mg). Nitro SL did not relieve his chest pain. The paramedics noticed STEMI (ST elevated MI) changes in the ECG. Their initial vital signs are: blood pressure is 168/92 mm Hg, the heart rate is 100 beats per minute, the respiratory rate is 14 breaths/minute, and the pulse oximetry reading is 97%. What is the next treatment and assessment you and your team should be performing?

b. Give morphine sulfate (MSO4) 2 to 4 mg for pain and draw blood specimens. Remember the pneumonic "MONA-B" (morphine, oxygen, nitro sl., aspirin and beta-blocker). Morphine can help with reducing pain and increasing cardiac perfusion. A non-contrast CAT scan would be done if he were having symptoms of a stroke. IV infusion of nitroglycerine is a secondary option if the pain is not relieved and the blood pressure remains stable. Do not use nitroglycerine if the patient has right ventricular infarction and dysfunction, or has recently taken dilating medications such as phosphodiesterase inhibitors (Viagra, for example), used for heart failure and erectile dysfunction. His best chance for recovery is having a percutaneous cardiac intervention.

47. When is the appropriate time to give Atropine 0.5 mg IV bolus/push?

b. Unstable bradycardia. Only when the patient is unstable is the appropriate time to use Atropine 0.5 mg. It is not a cardiac arrest drug. It is may not be effective in infranodal 2nd degree type II and third degree heart block. A transcutaneous or transvenous pacemaker with a vasoactive infusion may be necessary in the symptomatic heart blocks. Dopamine 2 to 10 mcg/kg/minute or Epinephrine 0.1 to 0.5 mcg/kg/minute are also recommended.

48. While treating a patient with dizziness, a blood pressure of 68/30 mm Hg, and cool, clammy skin, you see this lead II ECG rhythm. What rhythm is this and what is the treatment?

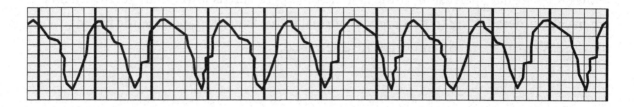

c. Monomorphic Ventricular Tachycardia - Synchronize cardioversion and Amiodarone 150 mg IVPB over 10 minutes. If needed, repeat the cardioversion, and consider adenosine with wide-complex tachycardia. It may be SVT.

49. You are caring for a patient with pneumonia who is orally intubated and is sedated and on a ventilator. The high-pressure alarm is sounding, what is your assessment and intervention?
b. Secretions accumulating; suction while pulling the catheter out; but not for more than 10 seconds. We often hyper-oxygenate before catheter insertion, and then suction. We do not hyperventilate the patient, which would lead to respiratory alkalosis. Waiting for the Respiratory Therapist to fix the problem may take too long.

50. What is the correct dose of aspirin for the patient complaining of chest pain?
b. 160 to 325 mg. This is the recommended dose. Chewable aspirin is often offered to the patient on the ambulance.

51. What is the lowest systolic blood pressure goal that guides the use of vasoactive medications and fluid boluses?

a. 90 mm Hg systolic. This is the usual criteria for the lowest systolic blood pressure that allows for adequate perfusion. If the systolic blood pressure is lower than 90, treatments are usually ordered. One to two liters of normal saline is used to increase the blood pressure. Vasoactive meds and drips are often used.

52. The team is hanging fluids for a patient post cardiac arrest to increase the blood pressure. What is the recommended initial fluid bolus?

d. 1 to 2 liters of isotonic or crystalloid fluid. In an emergency this is the initial fluid bolus. More fluids may be needed, as well as vasoconstricting medicated infusions. Sepsis protocols call for 20 to 30 ml/kg fluid boluses in the first hour.

53. Which treatments are no longer recommended during cardiac arrest?

c. Cricoid pressure, continuous 100% oxygen, atropine, vasopressin. Cricoid pressure during the compression cycles to prevent gastric distention is not effective, and can cause a gag reflex and vomiting. Too much 100% oxygen is toxic to the cell membranes, decreases cardiac output, cerebral blood flow and can also cause ocular damage. Atropine is not recommended in cardiac arrest, for it was found to be ineffective. Vasopressin was removed from the 2015 algorithms, because there was no benefit over epinephrine IVP, every 3 to 5 minutes.

54. Therapeutic Hypothermia, at 32 to 36 degrees celsius, often called "Code Chill" or Temperature Management has been used to treat patients' post-cardiac arrest. The ideal candidate for hypothermia protocol is which patient?

a. A victim who is resuscitated, but won't wake up. This is the candidate of choice for hypothermia treatment. If the cardiac arrest victim is awake or responding, they are no longer a candidate for the 24-hour hypothermia protocol.

55. The purpose of the 24-hour hypothermia protocol in the post cardiac arrest victim is . . . ?

a. Improving survival by reducing free radicals and decreasing oxygen demand. Reducing the demands in the brain is the benefit of hypothermia at the temperature of 32 to 36 degrees celsius (90 degrees F).

56. After the return of spontaneous circulation (ROSC), what are the emergency priorities?

a. Stabilize the vital signs, and transport the patient to a facility that can perform a percutaneous coronary angioplasty intervention (PCI). Door to balloon time is 90 minutes. Other priorities include cardiac testing, rule out stroke with a non-contrast CAT Scan, MRI, and other procedures.

57. You have been doing chest compressions on a victim in the cafeteria. Another employee brings over the Automatic External Defibrillator (AED). What should you tell the other rescuer?

d. Tell them to turn it on, and follow directions to apply pads. Compressions for 2 minutes and defibrillation gives the victim the best outcome.

58. The Automatic External Defibrillator (AED) does not analyze the victim's rhythm once you apply the pads. What is the next action to take?

c. Go back to fast and deep compressions.

59. The Emergency Medical Services (EMS) arrives on the scene of a traumatic cardiac arrest, where you have started CPR. There is an organized rhythm on the monitor but still no pulse. What are the causes of PEA?

c. Cardiac tamponade and tension pneumothorax. Other potentially treatable causes of cardiac arrest are: hypoxia, hypovolemia, hydrogen ions (acidosis), hypoglycemia, hypothermia, hyper/hypokalemia, toxins/tablets, thrombosis; coronary and pulmonary, and trauma.

60. The Emergency Medical Services (EMS) arrives with a patient in found unconscious after falling off a ladder. The patient is pulseless and remains in pulseless electrical activity. This prolonged situation continues as CPR continues with 3 more doses of epinephrine given. The team should be discussing the possibility of . . . ?

b. Tension pneumothorax. Tension pneumothorax and cardiac tamponade are possible in chest trauma, and needs to be treated urgently to get cardiac contractions to return. Terminating efforts is an appropriate consideration after a long code that results in asystole. Hypothermia protocol is only used in resuscitated victims who haven't responded. Atropine has been found ineffective in cardiac arrest rhythms.

61. A 92-year-old man is admitted to your unit. As you take his vital signs he has a loss of consciousness and you cannot feel a pulse. What needs to be done immediately?

a. Call the emergency response team and begin chest compressions. This is the first thing to do. The application of the AED/defibrillator pads and IV push epinephrine would be next in priorities in a cardiac arrest situation.

62. Once a victim is defibrillated, what is the first drug of choice in cardiac arrest?

b. Epinephrine 1 mg IV push. This is the drug of choice in cardiac arrest and after the defibrillation. Next is Amiodarone 300 mg IV push (can repeat at 150 mg IV push). "Shock-drug, shock-drug," with chest compressions fast and deep. Magnesium is used in magnesium deficiencies, or Torsades de Pointes.

63. Your victim collapsed at a wedding party. The team is doing compressions and you are ventilating. You are having a difficult time getting rise and fall of the chest. You ask for an oral airway. You are given a few choices. How will you select the correct size for the oral pharyngeal airway?

c. Measure the oral airway from the corner of the mouth/lip to the angle of the jaw near the ear. The nasopharyngeal airway is measured from the angle of the jaw to the tip of the victim's nose. These devices may help with ventilation and serve as a passageway for oxygen and a suction catheter.

64. When is a transcutaneous pacemaker recommended?

c. Unstable 3rd degree heart block. When the patient is experiencing symptoms and is becoming unstable due to a brady-arrhythmia, in particular 2nd degree, typr II, or 3rd degree heart block where atropine has not been effective. A pacemaker will be needed. There are pacemaker pads for the transcutaneous pacemaker, and another option is a central line, for insertion of the transvenous pacemaker.

65. Vagal maneuvers have not been effective for this patient in supraventricular tachycardia (SVT). The patient's blood pressure is stable. What is the dosing of adenosine for supraventricular tachycardia (SVT)?

b. 6 mg then 12 mg IV push fast, and flush. Adenosine is a naturally occurring nucleoside in the body. Given IVP, quickly, for its half-life is less than 10 seconds, causes dramatic effects as it slows the heart rate. It may initially cause 10 seconds of asystole.

66. Supraventricular tachycardia is caused by . . . ?

d. Reentry or re-excitation of an impulse. Reentry can possibly cause a heart rate to reach a rate above 150 bpm. Fever, dehydration, and anxiety all cause sinus tachycardia, with heart rates of 100 to 150 bpm.

67. If both the vagal maneuvers and adenosine is ineffective in resolving the patient's supraventricular tachycardia (SVT), the blood pressure is dropping, and the level of consciousness is changing, what is the next treatment of choice?

a. Synchronized cardioversion at 50 to 100 joules. If possible, sedation should be considered. Synchronized defibrillations shock the heart on the upstroke of the "R" wave, which avoids the sensitive "T" wave part of the cardiac cycle, avoiding the initiation of any deadly arrhythmias.

68. You are performing high quality CPR on an adult victim of cardiac arrest. Describe the compressions.

d. Both a and b. At two (2) to two and one half (2-1/2) inches deep, at least 100 to 120 compressions per minute. Use two hands, pressing on the lower half of the sternum.

69. At what points can the rescuer check a pulse on unconscious victims?

d. Both a and c. Check the pulse initially after calling the emergency services if you haven't already checked the pulse and at the 5 cycle two-minute compressor switch intervals.

70. Mrs. Cheeks is experiencing dizziness and weakness. Her cardiac monitor has a regular rhythm with a heart rate of 41. Her blood pressure had been 106/50, RR of 12, O2 saturation of 95%. You retake the blood pressure and it is 90/44. You see this rhythm on the monitor. What rhythm is displayed?

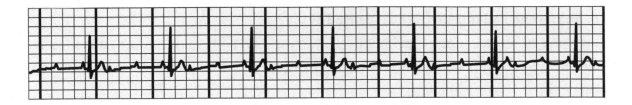

a. 2nd degree Type II (Mobitz II). The patient may become symptomatic and unstable.

71. What is the initial treatment to increase Mrs. Cheek's heart rate, and restore stability?

b. Atropine 0.5 mg IV push. This the recommended dose of Atropine, and initial recommended drug for unstable bradycardia. Atropine can be repeated every 3 to 5 minutes with a maximum dose of 3 mg. However, Atropine may not be effective in 2nd degree type II (Mobitz II), or 3rd degree heart block.

72. Initial treatments are not effective in increasing Mrs. Cheek's bradycardia. What are subsequent treatments to increase the patient's heart rate?

c. Transcutaneous pacemaker and a dopamine infusion. These are the next best choices for treatment of symptomatic bradycardia. Temporary transcutaneous pacemakers are usually available for victims on an ambulance or for patients in the hospital. A transvenous pacemaker, and permanent pacemakers, would be the next options for a complete heart block. Dobutamine may increase the heart rate but it will decrease the B/P as well. Cardizem will slow the heart rate and blood pressure, not increase it.

73. Which is a standard treatment procedure for patients with STEMI (ST elevated MI)?

a. Reperfusion therapy within 90 minutes. This is the treatment of choice for a victim of ST elevation myocardial infarction. Epinephrine would put a huge strain on the heart because it vasoconstricts and increases the heart rate. Morphine is a vasodilator, but it may drop the blood pressure if used in excess of 4 mg IVP. Defibrillation is used only in pulseless V-Fib or V-Tach.

74. The emergency personnel are treating a patient with symptomatic bradycardia. The team-leader asks for Atropine 1 mg IVP, and repeat every 3 to 5 minutes. You know the recommended dose is 0.5 mg every 3 to 5 minutes, with the maximum of 3 mg. You speak up in a professional manner to recommend the dose of 0.5 mg of Atropine, as in the 2015 ACLS guidelines. What is this behavior in team dynamics called?

b. Constructive Intervention. It is the professional manner in which to address and correct a team member, and team leader. Mutual Respect is behaving in a professional manner when discussing situations. Closed Loop Communication is repeating back the message to the team leader, to ensure the correct treatment when dosing or procedure is completed. Knowing one's limitations is performing within your scope of practice in which you are licensed, competent, and in one's job description.

75. An Ischemic stroke is . . . ?

a. The most common stroke, caused by a clot. 87% of strokes are caused by a clot, which is called an ischemic stroke. The "clot" stroke can be treated with a fibrinolytic tPA if timing is right. The bleed or hemorrhagic stroke (13%) is less common.

76. The emergency services will respond to a stroke victim and perform a stroke assessment on the victim. Which of the following is not one of the 3 assessments/tests the EMS uses to identify stroke?

d. Increase in hunger. Hunger is not an expected symptom of stroke. Slurred speech, arm drift, and facial droop, are the 3 assessments in the Cincinnati Stroke Scale. If one of those 3 tests are positive, the EMS knows that there is a 71% chance this victim is actually having a stroke.

77. What disorder can mimic the signs and symptoms of stroke?

b. Hypoglycemia. Hypoglycemia can mimic a stroke. Checking the patient's blood sugar may save time and unnecessary tests.

78. A routine test for patients who have had a stroke before they take any oral medications or liquids is . . . ?

b. Dysphagia and swallow screening. This is a simple test to ensure that the patient can swallow without aspiration. Sweat Test is for cystic fibrosis, Chvostek Sign tests for tetany seen in hypocalcemia. Sobriety Test is for drunk drivers.

79. The nasopharyngeal airway . . . ?

d. Both b and c. Is measured from the tip of the nose to the corner of the mandible, and provides a passageway for air between the nose and the pharynx. The nasopharyngeal airway is often used during a surgical procedure as a passageway for air in the unconscious patient. It is measured from the tip of the nose to the corner of the mandible or tragus of the ear.

80. What is the immediate and priority test required in the Emergency Department or Stroke Center for patients with signs and symptoms of a stroke?

b. Non-contrast CAT scan of the brain. The paramedics will radio ahead to the ED that a stroke patient is on the way. This is usually done within 25 minutes of arrival to the hospital. If the patient has signs and symptoms of a stroke, without any signs of hemorrhage on the CAT scan, the patient may meet the criteria for treatment with tPa.

81. The team began ventilations on a patient with respiratory distress. The ventilations delivered has improved the oxygenation, however the carbon dioxide level on the capnography monitor is 28. What direction would you give to the ventilator?

b. Slow down the ventilations to 10 to 12 bpm, to prevent hyperoxia, and reduction of cardiac output. Initial hyperventilation is effective, but the breaths need to be normalized to one breath every 5 to 6 seconds, to prevent oxygen free radicals, causing lung and brain complications.

82. Mr. Jenkins, a 67-year-old man, is brought into the ED. He has vague complaints of chest and arm pain. He had been nauseous earlier. The Emergency staff explains he may be having a heart attack. He is on a cardiac monitor, and has a peripheral IV. He is receiving oxygen and a pulse oximeter is attached. B/P is stable. What is the next priority?

b. 12-lead ECG. An ECG, while patient is stable, is the appropriate test to determine if and where in the myocardium there is ischemia. Continuous waveform capnography is used for procedural sedation or intubated patients and to determine if compressions are effective. Isuprel and Lidocaine infusions are not popular.

83. Mr. Neptune has premature ventricular contractions and short runs of ventricular tachycardia. What is the recommended medication to reduce the ventricular irritability?

c. Amiodarone 150 mg over 10 minutes. This is the initial dose of amiodarone. A continuous infusion will hopefully resolve the arrhythmias. Lidocaine 100 mg is an optional antiarrythmic. Aspirin 160 to 325 mg reduces the risk of clots in an MI, and epinephrine infusion will increase the work of the heart and the risk of arrhythmias.

84. Mr. Neptune is experiencing ventricular tachycardia. He is losing consciousness but has a pulse. What is the recommendation for cardioversion for this patient?

d. 100 synchronized joules. This is the safest and lowest amount of energy to successfully convert ventricular tachycardia with a pulse. The victim may need more joules if the intial cardioversion was unsuccessful.

85. To prepare for emergencies, what would be the correct steps for operating an AED?

b. Turn on the AED, apply pads, analyze the rhythm, clear the patient, deliver shock. Follow the AED prompts for a safe and effective defibrillation.

86. Mrs. Puff, an 85-year-old woman, is being evaluated for dizziness from a slow heart rate. You are measuring the PR interval on her ECG strip. Normally this interval is 0.12 to 0.20 seconds (3 to 5 small boxes). Her consistent but wide PR interval measures 11 little squares x .04 seconds = 0.44 seconds. What rhythm is she in?

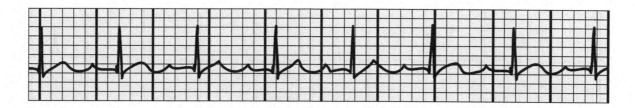

b. 1st degree AV block. 1st degree heart block patients usually remain stable and recover. Causes are usually myocardial infarction or ischemia, cardiac and anesthetic medications.

87. Mrs. Puff is still stable, but her heart rate decreases to 40 bpm. You notice an irregular rhythm and you re-measure the PR interval on her ECG strip. You notice the PR interval is getting longer and longer then drops a QRS. There are groupings of QRS's and then a P-wave without the QRS. What rhythm is she in now?

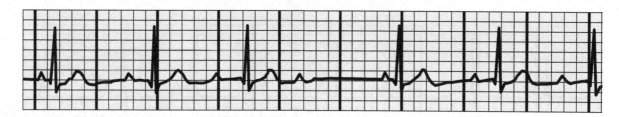

c. 2nd Degree AV block, type I, Mobitz I, (Wenckebach). This patient may not require immediate treatment. If they are unstable due to their slow heart rate, give Atropine 0.5 mg IV push every 3 to 5 minutes, maximum 3 mg.

88. Miss Karin is a patient in the cardiac care unit. In evaluating her ECG rhythm you notice a heart block because there are more P-waves than QRS waves. You notice that there isn't any relationship between the P-waves and the QRS waves. What rhythm is Mrs. Karin experiencing?

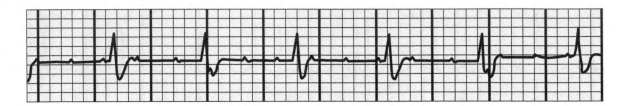

a. 3rd degree heart block. Also called Complete Heart Block or Atrial-Ventricular Dissociation. This rhythm may require a pacemaker and possibly a dopamine or epinephrine infusion.

89. Mr. Hazelton is a patient in the cardiac care unit. In evaluating his ECG rhythm you notice a slowing of the heart rate to 47 bpm. The rhythm is regular with narrow QRS's. You do not see any P-waves. What rhythm is Mr. Hazelton experiencing?

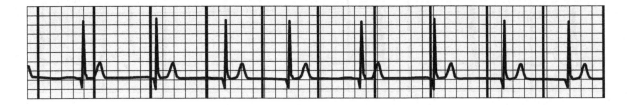

a. Junctional rhythm. There are no discernible P-waves. P-waves can be upside down before, after, or hidden in the QRS wave. The AV node fires between 40 and 60 bpm, where the patient may experience signs and symptoms of bradycardia.

90. In reviewing the heart blocks, you know that a 2nd degree type II (Mobitz II) heart block consists of . . . ?

d. All of the above. More P than Q waves, and narrow or wide QRS's. Every time there is a QRS wave, it is "married" to the P-wave and the PR intervals are consistent when they exist. These heart block patients can become symptomatic due to their bradycardia.

91. You are with the Rapid Response Team, and are called to the room of Mr. Simon, a 55-year-old male patient. He is awake but complaining of severe dizziness. His blood pressure is 94/40. Atropine has not worked. What is the next treatment of choice?

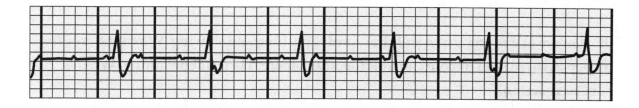

c. Transcutaneous pacemaker. If atropine is ineffective, the TCP or transvenous pacemaker is needed. Dopamine or epinephrine infusion may be needed. Magnesium is used if the electrolyte level is low. Hemodialysis and precordial thump are not treatments for 3rd degree heart block.

92. Mr. Simon needs immediate treatment for the hypotension caused by the above rhythm. What are the first considerations?

b. Pacemaker and a dopamine or epinephrine infusion. Amiodarone is for ventricular arrythmias, adenosine and cardioversion is for SVT. Fluids may be given to this patient, but should be given slowly to avoid causing CHF.

93. What is the correct dosing of Amiodarone in treating Ventricular Tachycardia with a pulse present?

c. Amiodarone 150 mg in 100 ml over 10 minutes. This is the correct dosing of Amiodarone when there is a pulse in a wide-complex tachycardia.

94. When the patient becomes unstable with a wide-complex tachycardia, what is the next treatment of choice?

c. Synchronized Cardioversion at 100 joules. This can be repeated and the joules increased. Press the "SYNC" button each time, when there is a pulse.

95. You are at a soccer game and the crowd is pushing and shoving. When the crowd disperses there is an unconscious victim near a fence. He is not breathing. What is your next action?

d. Both a and b. Call for assistance and check the victims pulse; and ensure that yourself and other rescuers are safe. Begin chest compressions if there is any doubt about finding a pulse. Call the EMS as quickly as possible.

96. You are caring for a patient who has been admitted to the hospital for rapid atrial fibrillation. The cardiologist has tried to treat the patient with calcium channel blockers. But the fast heart rate is now causing the blood pressure to drop as well. The team is preparing to sedate and synchronize cardiovert. How many joules will the cardiologist request?

b. 120 to 200 joules. This is the 2015 recommended amount of joules for rapid atrial fibrillation. For SVT, 50 to 100 joules is recommended. A-Fib may be a stubborn rhythm to convert.

97. You are caring for the patient pre-procedure. He complains of feeling his heart racing. Vital signs are B/P 112/64, HR 168, RR 12, pulse oximetry 95%. His lungs are clear and the 12-lead ECG has been repeated. What are the best options for the team are in providing care for this patient?

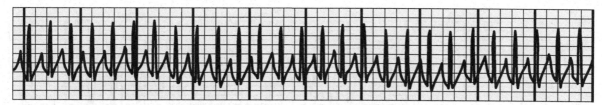

d. All of the above. Look at the ECG to determine if the QRS's are narrow or wide. If wide it can be SVT or V-Tach with a pulse. Also consider cardioversion if the patient becomes unstable. And consider vagal maneuvers, adenosine, and contact a cardiologist.

98. The team has the pads on the cardiac arrest victim's chest, the defibrillator is charging, chest compressions continue until the team leader ensures patient and team safety by stating I'm going to shock on three. One, two, three, everyone clear. What happens after the shock is delivered?

b. The team returns to doing compressions. Unless the team sees other signs of life and perfusion it is not recommended to take the time to check pulses. Even if there is a pulse, it may not be effective. Chest compressions is the best option. The routine is shock-drug-shockdrug, not consecutive defibrillations

99. You are assigned to care for Mr. Pabst, a patient in the Emergency Department. He is drowsy, but easy to arouse, and appears intoxicated. His history reveals alcoholism, hypertension, and an old ECG on file shows prolonged Q-T intervals. The cardiac monitor alarm alerts you to an arrhythmia. What is the rhythm below?

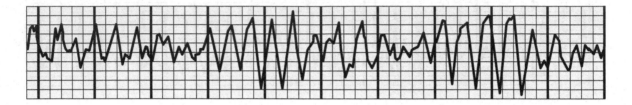

a. Torsades de Pointes (Polymorphic V-Tach). This is the polymorphic form of ventricular tachycardia that this patient is experiencing. Magnesium may be the first drug given.

100. Mr. Star's vital signs remain stable despite the continuing dysrhythmia present on the cardiac monitor. The emergency department team is preparing for cardioversion and applies the pads to his chest. In the meantime, as the team leader, what treatment would you want for this patient?

b. Magnesium 1 to 2 grams, IV fast infusion. Magnesium IV infusion over a few minutes is the appropriate drug for Torsade de Pointes, often caused by magnesium deficiencies. Amiodarone would be the next appropriate antiarrhythmic to be given (150 mg over 10 minutes). Adenosine 6 then 12 mg IV push is used primarily for narrow complex tachycardia, like SVT. Dobutamine and dopamine infusions are used to control blood pressure and cardiac output in critically ill patients.

101. Ms. Pearl is brought into the emergency department by the EMS. She had pulled her car over to the side of the road, and she slumped over and went ito cardiac arrest. EMS was called and bystanders intitiated effective chest compressions. The paramedics arrived and defibrillated Mrs. Pearl back into a sinus rhythm. The team is now discussing the initiation of the hyperthermia temperature management protocol. What is the recommendations for temperature management?

c. 32 to 36 degrees Celsius for 24 hours. The temperature management should be started within 6 hours of resuscitation, and maintained for 24 hours.

Notes

Part 4:
The Appendix

Notes

Glossary

Amiodarone (Cordarone): antiarrhythmic agent used for various types of cardiac dysrhythmias, both ventricular and atrial.

Anaphylaxis: a serious allergic reaction that is rapid in onset and may cause death. It typically causes a number of symptoms including an itchy rash, throat swelling, and low blood pressure.

Angina: chest pain due to ischemia of the heart muscle, generally due to obstruction or spasm of the coronary arteries. The main cause of angina pectoris is coronary artery disease, due to atherosclerosis of the arteries feeding the heart.

Antiarrhythmic Agents: a group of pharmaceuticals that are used to suppress abnormal rhythms of the heart (cardiac arrhythmias), such as atrial fibrillation, atrial flutter, ventricular tachycardia, and ventricular fibrillation.

Asystole: also known as flatline, is a state of no cardiac electrical activity, no contractions of the myocardium, and no cardiac output or blood flow. Prolonged asystole is an indicator for a medical practitioner to certify clinical or legal death.

Atrial Fibrillation (A-fib): the most common cardiac arrhythmia (heart rhythm disorder) caused by multipe irritable foci in the atrium. It may not cause symptoms, but it is often associated with palpitations, fainting, chest pain, congestive heart failure and stroke.

Atrial Flutter: caused by one irritable foci in the atrium. An abnormal heart rhythm usually associated with a fast heart rate or tachycardia (beats over 100 per minute).

Atropine: dilates the pupils, increases heart rate, and reduces salivation and other secretions. Used in unstable bradycardia.

Beta-Adrenergic Blockers: interfere with the binding to the receptor of epinephrine and other stress hormones, and weaken the effects of stress hormones. Used for the management of cardiac arrhythmias, protecting the heart from a heart attack (myocardial infarction), arrythmias and hypertension.

Bi-Phasic: a type of defibrillation waveform where a shock is delivered to the heart via two vectors.

Bigeminy: an arrhythmia in which abnormal heart beats occur every other beat.

Bolus: the administration of a drug, medication, or other substance, in the form of a single, small, or large dose, over a short period of time.

Bradycardia: is the resting heart rate of under 50 beats per minute (BPM), although it is seldom symptomatic, it is treated with atropine, pacemaker and positive chronotropic drugs.

Calcium Channel Blockers: a chemical that disrupts the movement of calcium through calcium channels. Used as antihypertensive drugs, (decrease blood pressure).

Capnography (PETCO2): is the monitoring of the concentration or partial pressure of carbon dioxide in the respiratory gases. Used to monitor ventilation in the Operating Room and patients that are sedated for procedures. Can also determine if chest compressions are effective.

Chronotropic: changing the heart rate.

Cardiac Tamponade (pericardial tamponade/effusion): a serious condition in which fluid accumulates around the heart.

Cardiogenic Shock: is based upon an inadequate circulation of blood due to primary failure of the ventricles of the heart to function effectively.

Cincinnati Prehospital Stroke Scale: a 3-step assessment used to diagnose the presence of a stroke in a patient. (Slurred speech, facial drooping, arm weakness or drift.)

Commotio Cordis: (agitation of the heart) is a lethal disruption of the cardiac rhythm that occurs as a result of a blow to the area directly over the heart at a critical time during the cardiac cycle causing cardiac arrest.

Depolarization: a positive-going change in a cell's membrane potential, making it more positive, or less negative.

Dopamine: a medicated infusion that can increase the blood pressure and heart rate.

Endotracheal Tube: a specific type of tracheal tube that is inserted through the mouth (orotracheal), or nose (nasotracheal), to deliver oxygen.

Epinephrine: adrenaline; hormone; regulates heart rate and causes vasoconstriction; is used as a drug to treat cardiac arrest and other cardiac dysrhythmias resulting in diminished or absent cardiac output. Also used to treat severe allergic reactions.

Glasgow Coma Scale (GCS): a neurological scale that gives a way of recording the conscious state of a person.

Heart Block: interruptions in electrical conduction through the heart due to ischemic or diseased cardiac tissue.

Hyperkalemia: elevated potassium.

Hypoglycemia: extremely low blood sugar/glucose.

Hypokalemia: low potassium.

Hypothermia: low body temperature.

Hypothermia Protocol (Temperature Management): chilling of the unconscious, resuscitated, post cardiac arrest victim's body for 24 hours, at 32 to 36 degrees celcius to decrease neurological damage.

Hypovolemia: decreased blood volume.

Hypoxia: a pathological condition in which the body, or a region of the body, is deprived of an adequate oxygen supply.

Infusion Therapy: involves the administration of medication through a needle or catheter.

Inotropic: increasing the contractility of the heart.

Intraosseous Infusion (IO): use of a drill, or hand held needle, to access the bone marrow of the tibia or humerous. IV fluids, blood and drugs can then be delivered into the central circulation.

Ischemia: a restriction in blood supply to tissues, causing a shortage of oxygen and glucose needed for cellular metabolism.

Joules: a unit of energy; e.g. 200 J, or 200 joules.

Junctional/Nodal Rhythm: an abnormal heart rhythm resulting from impulses coming from the area of the atrioventricular node, the "junction" between atria and ventricles.

LMA (Laryngeal Mask Airway): an inflatable mask like device inserted into the hypopharynx, without the use of a laryngoscope. Used in anesthesia and emergency medicine, for a short-term intubation/airway.

MERCI Procedure (Mechanical Embolus Removal in Cerebral Ischemia): used to remove blood clots from the brain of people suffering strokes. The device is a tiny corkscrew sent to the brain through a femoral artery catheter to remove the clot.

Mobitz/Wenckebach: name of heartblocks causing bradycardia.

MONA-B: mnemonic for Morphine, Oxygen, Nitrates, Aspirin and Beta Blocker, which are drugs used initially in acute coronary syndromes.

MOVIE: mnemonic for Monitor, Oxygen, Vitals Signs, IV, and 12-lead ECG.

Nasal Cannula: a device used to deliver supplemental oxygen via the nostrils.

Norepinephrine / Levophed: a medication similar to epinephrine, acts to constrict blood vessels (increase B/P and HR) in medical emergencies.

Oximetry / Pulse oximetry: a non-invasive method for monitoring a patient's O2 saturation.

Pacemaker: is a device that sends impulses to the heart to control abnormal rhythms. It can be an implanted device, a wire threaded into the vasculature to the internal heart wall, or impulses sent through external pads placed on the chest.

Percutaneous Coronary Intervention (PCI): coronary angioplasty is a procedure (balloon/stent) used to treat the stenotic (narrowed) coronary arteries of the heart found in coronary heart disease.

PEA (Pulseless Electrical Activity): (electromechanical dissociation): refers to a cardiac arrest situation in which a heart rhythm is observed on the electrocardiogram, but no cardiac output or pulse is produced.

Phosphodiesterase Inhibitor: A cardiovascular drug that vasodilates, increases organ perfusion, and decreases systemic vascular resistance. The drug lowers blood pressure. The drug is used to treat heart failure patients. The vasodilation effect makes it a popular drug to treat male erectile dysfunction.

Post-Mortem Lividity: purplish discoloration or settling of the blood in the lower dependent portions of the dead body, after 2 to 3 hours. Discoloration does not occur in body parts that have contact with the ground or other objects, where capillaries are compressed.

PR Interval: in the electrocardiogram, the time elapsing between the beginning of the P-wave and the beginning of the next QRS complex. It is normally 0.12 to 0.20 seconds, and up to 5 small boxes on the rhythm strip.

Quadrigeminy: a form of cardiac arrhythmia in which every fourth beat is a Premature Ventricular Contraction.

Q Waves: a sign of previous myocardial infarction. They may be found in the 12-lead ECG (a downward deflection after the P-wave).

Recoil: is the act of relieving the pressure off the chest after each compression, allowing the heart to refill.

QRS Wave: Ventricular depolarization. Waveform normally measures 0.06 to 0.20 seconds.

ST Elevation: in a 12-lead ECG, if the ST segments are abnormally high above the isoelectric line, an acute MI is suspected.

Rigor Mortis: one of the recognizable signs of death, caused by chemical changes in the muscles after death, causing the limbs of the corpse to become stiff and difficult to move or manipulate.

Renal Replacement Therapy: a term used to encompass life-supporting treatments for renal failure.

STEMI: ST Elevated Myocardial Infarction on the ECG.

Supraventricular Tachycardia (SVT): rapid heart rhythm, above 150 bpm originating at or above the atrioventricular node.

Synchronized Cardioversion: an electrical shock using the defibrillator, to slow down an unstable patient's fast heart rate (tachycardia), or ventricular dysrhythmias.

Tachycardia: a heart rate that exceeds the normal range. Usually over 100 bpm.

Transcutaneous Pacemaker (TCP): a pacemaker that speeds up a patient's heart through two pads that are applied to the bare chest and back. Energy passes through the skin and chest wall, stimulating the heart muscle.

Tension-Pneumothorax: the progressive build-up of air within the pleural space, usually due to a lung laceration which allows air to escape into the pleural space but not to escape. Pressure builds up, and can cause cardiac compression and arrest. The emergency treatment is a needle aspiration or chest tube to remove the air or blood.

Transcutaneous: refers to medications applied directly to the skin (transdermal creams or ointments), or in time-release forms (skin patches).

Transvenous Pacemaker: a pacemaker wire that is threaded through a central line into the ventrical to stimulate and speed up the heart rate. There is an external pacemaker box controlling the heart rate.

Trigeminy: a form of cardiac arrhythmia in which every third beat is a premature ventricular contraction.

Vagal Maneuver / Valsalva Maneuver: holding your breath and bearing down. It is performed by the patient experiencing fast heart rates. This maneuver stimulates the vagus nerve, causing the heart rate to slow down. Often medications are needed as well.

Vasopressin: antidiuretic hormone; secreted by the posterior lobe of the pituitary gland that constricts blood vessels, raises blood pressure, and reduces excretion of urine. Vasopressin was removed from the guidelines in October 2015, because there was no benefit over epinephrine every 3 to 5 mintes. (The adult dose in cardiac arrest for vasoconstriction purposes was 40 units IV push.)

Ventricular Fibrillation: a condition in which there is chaotic movement of the ventricles in the heart, making them quiver rather than contract properly. Ventricular fibrillation is the most commonly identified arrhythmia in cardiac arrest patients. Automatic external defibrillators are effective life saving devices outside the hospital setting for this arrythmia.

Ventricular Tachycardia (VT, V-Tach): a fast heart rhythm, that originates in one of the ventricles of the heart, can be life threatening. Patient can have a pulse, and become unstable, or can be pulseless and it is treated as Ventricular Fibrillation.

About The Authors

Michele G. Kunz, MSN, ANP, RN-BC

Michele is a Certified Instructor and specializes in providing Certification classes in ACLS, BLS, and PALS. Visit her website to see more about her classes, books, study guides, essays, and articles. Visit Michele's YouTube page to see all of her free video lessons.

Michele has been a clinical nursing educator for over 32 years. During those years, she has helped many thousands of nurses improve their own job performance and increase their own job satisfaction. Michele considers herself to be a nurse's nurse, because she is not hidden away in a classroom or office, but out on the floor everyday – interacting with hospital management, the nurses, the patients, and the physicians.

For many years Kunz was the Director of Nursing Education and Informatics at Long Island College Hospital in Brooklyn, NY. She was in the LICH Nursing Education Department for 25 years. Kunz developed the desire to teach nurses over 30 years ago when she was an ICU nurse at Staten Island Hospital (now called SI University Hosptial). It was at SIH that Kunz realized that she could learn how to be a better nurse by teaching the other nurses. Kunz hasn't stopped teaching since then.

Kunz is now the Critical Care Educator at Mercy Medical Center in Rockville Centre, Long Island, NY.

She is also the Director of Education at Dickson Keanaghan, LLC, a company that she helped create, where Michele and Joe train and certify the medical staff of over 600 hospitals, medical offices, and surgi-centers on Long Island, New York City, and Westchester. If you would like to take one of her classes, or have her come to your office and train your staff, please visit her training website at MicheleKunz.com. Connect with Michele on LinkedIn at http://www.linkedin.com/in/nursingeducatormichelegkunz

Joseph C. Kunz, Jr., MBA, BA

When Joe and Michele met in 1984, Michele was working full-time in the Intensive Care Unit at Staten Island University Hospital, and teaching a few classes on the side. Joe was building his first start-up company on Long Island, and began assisting Michele with the classes. By 1985 they realized that they wanted to take their little part-time training business to the next level. So, the two of them took a part-time weekend job at a nursing service in Brooklyn where they taught certification classes to nurses and physicians. Michele taught the classes, and Joe learned all about managing the business, the classes, the students, the classroom, the other instructors, and the equipment.

Eventually the Kunz's started to teach more classes on their own. They very quickly built a dedicated following of nurses and physicians throughout New York City and Long Island. They then started to grow the company very quickly and began training and certifying the medical staff at medical offices and then entire hospitals.

The Kunz's business would not be as successful as it is without the both of them working together. Right from the beginning Joe brought all his business experience and entrepreneurial fortitude into the operation. Joe had been developing his business skills and work-ethic from a very young age. He has worked very hard at making the business professional, successful, and strong. Over these last 32 years, Michele has perfected the teaching part of our operation, and Joe has perfected the marketing, management, and financial side.

The Kunz's business has been a wonderful 32+ year learning experience and journey. Despite the long days and hard work, they never want their journey to end. Each are looking forward to seeing how far they can take it. The more healthcare professionals and students that they help, the more successful they both feel. Joseph is a Certified Instructor for BLS. Connect with Joe on LinkedIn at www.linkedin.com/in/josephckunzjr/

AMERICAN *inspirations*

by MARY JANE TIFFANY

MEDICAL EDUCATORS WITH *Heart*

(and business brains)

Michele and Joe Kunz have created a business based on their love of teaching, helping others be successful, and for being together. Michele proudly says "teaching and sharing information is our life's mission."

Together they have been on the front-line of teaching and certifying healthcare professionals and students since 1984. They saw that there was a great need for educators that loved their subject matter, and that would treat their students with the respect they deserved. They have since built their medical training company into one of New York City's and Long Island's most popular American Heart Association certification companies. They train and certify the medical staff at over 600 hospitals, surgicenters, medical offices, and universities.

Michele has been in nursing education for over 30 years. She is also the Director of Nursing Education at Mercy Medical Center on Long Island. Joe has been a business innovator and entrepreneur for over 30 years. He has been building and managing their business and finding and creating new and better ways to reach out and help more healthcare professionals be successful.

Over the years their classroom study materials developed a large national following. "In the early days we were creating, using, and distributing our own study materials before any existed in the marketplace," Joe recalls. "Healthcare professionals and students were desperate for easy-to-use study materials. So we created them." In 2003 they finally decided to branch into publishing with their *Zombie Notes*® study charts and books. They have been national best-sellers for the last several years.

The Kunzs have built their careers on providing fun, practical, timely, and informative classes, study materials, and videos that assist healthcare professionals and students in making our world a better place to live. Clearly, the art of educating is their passion, and it is one that Michele and Joe Kunz cherish. ∎

TheNurseEducator.com
MicheleKunz.com

Mary Jane Tiffany is a business professor at a major university in Texas and the author of several entrepreneurship books. She writes extensively on entrepreneurial couples.

About Dickson Keanaghan

Our Medical Training Adventure Begins

We developed the *Zombie Notes Study Charts* in 1984, when we first started teaching certification classes in New York City. Back then, there were no practical or effective study guides for our students to use or buy. So we had to develop our own study material to help prepare our students for the classes. We very quickly learned what works with our students and what doesn't. Our classes and study guides very quickly developed a very large local audience in Manhattan and Brooklyn.

The nurses and physicians in our classes would then call us to come to their offices and hospitals to train and certify their entire staff as well as individual departments. We now train the medical staff at over 600 hospitals, surgi-centers, medical offices, walk-in medial offices, major drug stores, and military bases throughout Long Island, New York City, and Westchester. We also train and certify medical students, and students in the allied health professions, at several colleges and universities. Many continue to come from different parts of the country to take our classes.

Our Publishing Adventure Begins

As our students moved around the country, our study guides went with them. This national exposure created a demand for our study guides throughout the fifty states and eventually the entire English speaking world. This demand was just the push we needed to start our own publishing company. As college nursing professors, students, and hospital education departments from around the country began calling us requesting to purchase our study guides, we began printing them at home and sending them out as fast as physically possible.

But the demand became too great and too time consuming. So we then hired a professional printing company to print them for us in large quantities. Luckily, the internet came along, and then the new-media publishing revolution began. So we jumped in with both feet and with our eyes and ears wide open.

Dedication

• We dedicate this book to healthcare professionals everywhere who have dedicated their life to helping those in need; and,

• To healthcare students who do not yet realize the potential and importance of the career they have chosen; and,

• To our students all over Long Island and New York City (and those that have spread out over the 50 states), and our readers, including the American military medical personnel, all over the world, that work every day at making their career a success and our world a much better place in which to live; and,

• Finally, we dedicate this book to you all with our love, appreciation, and thanks for allowing us to be a part of your lives.

Legal Disclaimer

This book is presented solely for educational purposes for healthcare professionals and healthcare students. This book is not meant to be used by non-healthcare persons, nor should it be used to diagnose or treat any medical condition. For diagnosis or treatment of any medical problem, consult your own physician. The publisher and authors are not responsible for any specific health needs that may require medical supervision and are not liable for any damages or negative consequences from any treatment, action, application, or preparation, to any person reading or following the information in this book. Neither the American Heart Association (AHA), nor the American Red Cross (ARC), endorse this publication.

References are provided for informational purposes only and do not constitute endorsement of any websites or other sources. Readers should be aware that the websites and links listed in this book may change at any time, and without notice.

Bibliography

Sinz, Elizabeth, ed. (2015). *ACLS for Experienced Providers: Manual and Resource Text.* American Heart Association.

Kunz, Michele G. (2013). *Zombie Notes Study Charts: ACLS Vocabulary.* Dickson Keanaghan, LLC.

Kunz, Michele G. (2016). *Zombie Notes Study Charts: ACLS Certification Exam Prep.* Dickson Keanaghan, LLC.

Acknowledgements

In preparing to write this acknowledgments section, a flood of memories came back to me of the many people that were part of my development as a nurse and nursing educator. I have been developing my skills as a nurse, and nurse educator, for over 32 years. And I still continue to develop my skills every day. I would like to tell you about some of the people that played an important part of my professional development.

My first CPR and first-aide course was at The College of Staten Island, in New York City, (then it was called Staten Island Community College), taught by Ira Sweet, in 1976. To this day I use his teaching techniques to motivate my students to be successful healthcare professionals. He inspired me, and everyone in the class, by including real-life on-the-job stories into his lecture.

When I became an ICU nurse at Staten Island Hospital, in New York City, in 1980, I had the opportunity to work with and learn from many highly skilled critical care nurses. The one that stood out the most was my nursing preceptor Laura Gasparis-Von Frolio. She was a very dynamic patient-advocate and a brilliant nurse. After taking a four-day AHA-BLS Instructor Course at Beth Israel Medical Center, in New York City, in 1984, Gasparis and I began to teach classes to dental and medical offices and to the community. We called our little training company CPR Associates.

I loved teaching these classes and wanted to teach many more. Luckily, in 1984, my SIH-ICU co-worker and friend Rosemary Egitto-Burda read about an open position for CPR Coordinator at Long Island College Hospital, in Brooklyn. I interviewed for this position and was accepted. I was to remain at LICH at an educator for the next 25 years (my first 13 years as a Staff-Development Instructor and CPR Coordinator; my last 12 years as Director of Nursing Education and Informatics).

During my time at LICH, 1984-2009, I was also involved in American Heart Association (AHA) program developments as a Committee Member at The Regional Emergency Medical Services Council, of NY (REMSCO). It was the only Community Training Center (CTC) in NYC at the time (1980's). Names that stand out from those days are Nancy and George Benedetto, Virginia Klunder, Mary Gallagher, and Ed Stapleton. Our group looked at the evidence-based practice and science to develop the best training programs for NY trainers in ACLS, BLS, and PALS. This organization also provided guidelines for the New York City EMS services.

I would especially like thank to my LICH co-workers in the Nursing Education Department: Esme Elisson, RN-NP, Emergency Department Clinical Nurse Specialist; Lorraine Woltman, RN; and, and Louisa Travers, RN. I worked closely with these amazingly talented nursing educators teaching the nurses and other healthcare professionals for 25 years. Many of these years included the late Lynn Hahn, RN. Lynn was a very experienced and professional nurse whose skills I always admired.

I am especially proud of Robin Ndiaye, the administrative secretary for the Nursing Department. She also took the BLS Instructor Course and has been teaching CPR to the staff and community for many years. These woman would flex their hours and work with manikins on the floor for hours and hours in order to get our staff certified. We would then clean the manikins for another two hours – and we always had a good time doing it together.

I would also like to thank my good friend and fellow nurse Christine Molinari. We started together in critical care on Staten Island. And, coincidentally, both of our families moved out to Long Island to work and live. We teach many, many classes together. She always brings great humor, and a great work ethic, to all of my classes. Christine has always made my students feel comfortable and relaxed with a friendly learning environment.

More than anyone else, I must thank my best friend and husband, Joseph. When Joe and I met in 1984, I was working full-time in the Intensive Care Unit at Staten Island Hospital, in New York City, and teaching a few classes in Brooklyn and Queens, on the side. Joe was building his first start-up company on Long Island, and assisting me with the classes. Around 1988 the two of us took a part-time job at B & G, a nursing service in Brooklyn, where we taught certification classes to nurses and physicians. I taught the classes, and Joe learned about managing the business, the classes, the students, the classroom, the other instructors, and the equipment.

Eventually we started to teach more classes on our own. We very quickly built a dedicated following of nurses and physicians throughout New York City and Long Island. We then started to grow the company very quickly by training and certifying the medical staff at several medical offices - and then entire hospitals. Amazingly, we now train and certify medical professionals and students in over 600 hospitals, medical offices, surgi-centers, universities, and military bases, throughout Long Island, New York City, and Westchester.

Our business would not be as successful as it is without the both of us working together. Right from the beginning Joe brought all his business experience and entrepreneurial fortitude into our operation. Joe had been developing his business skills and work-ethic from a very young age. He has worked very hard at making our business professional, successful, and strong. Over these last 32 years, I have perfected the teaching part of our operation, and he has perfected the marketing, management, and financial side.

He is also the one that makes it possible for our little training business to reach out and connect with many thousands of healthcare professionals every day of the year, all over the world. He has an amazing ability to put all the information I throw at him into a practical and beautiful format. He is able to make our publications, websites, and videos, in such a way that our students are able learn the material with ease.

Joe has been our business manager since 1984. In 2003, we expanded our business once again, and named it Dickson Keanaghan, which are names from Joe's family. Joe became the President and CEO of our new corporation, and he officially became Director of Operations for our training company. In these roles he is responsible for all finance, marketing, and business development. Our business has been a wonderful 32 year learning experience and journey.

Michele G. Kunz
Long Island, New York

Praise For The *Zombie Notes Study Charts* And For Michele And Her Classes

"Michele's YouTube videos were terrific! Clear, concise, and very helpful. The *Zombie Notes* are the best way to study and review this information - and actually learn it. The groupings and mnemonics make it easy to apply in real patient situations. In Michele's class I actually learned pertinent facts that translate into real practice. It really doesn't get any better than Michele's class - quick, convenient, and very meaningful."
Denise May, RN, Winthrop University Hospital, Mineola, NY

"I took Michele's class with all of my co-workers here at our office. I loved the *Zombie Notes Study Charts*. They were very helpful. Michele has a great personality and is perfect for teaching nurses. I really enjoyed her class and I look forward to taking her other classes."
Erin Cunningham, RN, Long Island Lung Center, Bay Shore, NY

"The YouTube videos were great. I have been to Michele's classes in the past. The *Zombie Notes Study Charts* were short, concise, and to the point, but full of pertinent information. I like that Michele provided us with the Zombie Notes. Michele is full of practical and useful information and very funny."
Kate Burke, RN, Cohen Children's Medical Center of New York, New York City, NY

"Michele's videos were the first time I was seeing ECG strips. Because of her videos, I showed up to her class well prepared. They helped make the class much easier to understand. I rewrote the *Zombie Notes* twice to help memorize them. By going back and re-reading what I wrote, while watching the videos, was helping me to understand them. I am applying for my clinical ladder and Michele's class was a requirement. I am glad I learned this material. Michele kept the class fun and interesting. The notes and slides were broken down into very easy to understand segments."
Christine Chambers, Good Samaritan Hospital, West Islip, NY

"Michele's program has an excellent presentation and an enjoyable format. Her program is interactive and an excellent discussion that can't be offered by a computer-based program."
Dr. Paul Epstein, NAPA, North Shore - Long Island Jewish Medical Center, Manhasset, NY

"I have already been to Michele's classes three times. The *Zombie Notes* are the best memorization guide available. Michele is also the best educator around, by far. We ask her to teach our office every time."
Dr. Steven Macharola, Island Eye Surgi-Center, Carle Place, NY

"I watched Michele's videos. They helped me know what to expect and how to prepare for class. I have been to Michele's classes in the past. I loved the *Zombie Notes*. Everyone I know uses them to study for the PA boards. I liked the pace of Michele's class, and the hands-on-experience we gained."
Samantha Prinzing, PA, Montefiorc Hospital, Manhattan, NY

"Michele's videos were awesome. My friends at Brookhaven Hospital told me about Michele's classes. The *Zombie Notes* were also awesome. They really helped me retain the information. The class was excellent and I learned a lot. The class is very concise and informative. Michele is a great instructor. Thank you Michele."
Ken Daniels, RN, Jamaica Hospital, Queens, NY

"I learned about Michele's classes from a co-worker. The videos were very helpful in understanding the material. Michele made the class a lot of fun, but we also gained a lot of knowledge. Michele had an excellent knowledge of the material and was able to help me understand the info."
Sandra Fernandez, RN, Long Island Center for Digestive Health, Garden City, NY

"I learned about Michele's classes from a co-worker. Her *Zombie Notes* were great - brief and to the point. Michele was very easy to understand. I felt much more confident in the subject matter by the time I finished her class. I loved Michele's class so much. I felt more relaxed than when I first took ACLS with a different instructor."
Doreen Cooney, RN, Nassau University Medical Center, East Meadow, NY

"I have taken Michele's classes in the past and returned to take her ACLS class again. Her class was informative, timely, and very pertinent."
Barbara Kusky, RN, Bay Pines VA Hospital, Bay Pines, FL

"Michele's class is concise, to the point, very informative, and very entertaining."
Laurie Savoia, RN, Long Island Center for Digestive Health, Garden City, NY

"I come to Michele Kunz every time I need an ACLS class because she is the greatest instructor, educator, teacher, nursing brain to ever walk on the planet."
Andrea LaFata, RN, Nursing Supervisor, Good Samaritan Hospital, West Islip, NY

"I liked Michele's YouTube videos very much. They were very informative. After watching, everything began to "click", and I began to understand much more. Michele was very informative, and student friendly. She is very geared to teaching and helping, not failing people."
Laura Monas, RN, Cohen's Children's Medical Center Of New York, at Long Island Jewish Medical Center, Lake Success, NY

"Michele's YouTube videos made it very easy for me to prepare for the class. The *Zombie Notes Study Charts* were excellent, and highlighted all the important information. Michele is very personable, and made learning the material less stressful."
Madaline Safrey, RN, St. Joseph's Hospital, Bethpage, NY

"I liked Michele's YouTube videos. The *Zombie Notes Study Charts* were very helpful. Her class is very interactive and very friendly. Everything was excellent."
Dr. Araz Ibragimov, Kings County Hospital, Brooklyn, NY

"The *Zombie Notes Study Charts* were an excellent study guide. It goes straight to the important stuff."
Dr. Yimar Berrios, Kings County Hospital, Brooklyn, NY

"Thank you very much Michele! I always look forward to your classes. You truly have a gift. Making people laugh and enjoy learning at the same time is a beautiful thing."
Rosemary Fine, RN North Shore-Long Island Jewish Medical Center, Lake Success, NY

"My nursing professor Cathy Jansen at Nassau Community College recommended that I take Michele's class for ACLS. Professor Jansen has previously taken Michele's ACLS class. I really enjoyed Michele's YouTube videos tremendously. And her *Zombie Notes Study Charts* were also a great way to comprehend the study material beforehand. As a student nurse, I have a great interest in critical care, which is Michele's specialty. Michele is phenomenal. Her class was broken up between the lecture, the video, the multiple choice test, and the hands-on exam."
Jessica Joseph, Nursing student at Nassau Community College, Garden City, NY

"Michele's YouTube videos were terrific! Clear, concise, and very helpful. The *Zombie Notes Study Charts* are the best way to study and review this information – and actually learn it. The groupings and mnemonics make it easy to apply in real patient situations. In Michele's class I actually learned pertinent facts that translate into real practice. It really doesn't get any better than Michele's class – quick, convenient, and meaningful."
Denise May, Winthrop University Hospital, Mineola, NY

Request For Testimonials

We are looking for short testimonials about this book to be used in all of our promotional material, on our websites, and possibly here in this book.

It should be a three to five sentence statement about this book and how it has helped you with passing the certification exam. Please be as specific and as detailed as possible. You can see examples of great testimonials inside this book.

Please include your name, title, hospital or company name, and town and state. You are also welcome to include a small picture of yourself, as well as a link to your website.

You can quickly and easily send us your testimonial by email at:
MKunz@TheNurseEducator.com.

By sending us your testimonial, you are giving us permission to use it in any and all of our advertising and marketing programs.

Thank you very much. We greatly appreciate your help with this.

Joe & Michele Kunz

"I just completed Michele's ACLS and BLS certification classes. I loved the *Zombie Notes Study Charts*. They streamlined the key facts needed to provide effective ACLS and BLS to my patients – and were a big help when preparing for the class and exam. I also enjoyed Michele's YouTube videos. I was very impressed with how easy Michele's videos made it for me to understand the topics we needed to know about for the class. Michele's class was very relaxed, yet very professional."
Linda Stio, RN, Neurological Surgery, PC, Long Island, NY

Colophon

- Interior text originally created in MS Word
- Final book designed and created in Adobe InDesign CC
- All fonts from Adobe Typekit

- All text and bullets set in Adobe Caslon Pro
- Page headers set in Myriad Pro
- Graphics and cover created in Adobe Illustrator CC

- Cover colors created in Adobe Color CC
- Cover fonts are Trajan Pro 3, and Myriad Pro
- Photographs created in Adobe Photoshop CC

- Finished book and cover converted to PDF using Adobe Acrobat Pro DC
- CIP data block created by librarian and publisher Adrienne Bashista, cipblock.com
- Trademarks handled by attorney Kelly Talcott, kdtalcott.com

- Paperback book printed and bound by Lightning Source
- Paperback book distibution by Lighning Source and Ingram
- Online retail sales by Amazon

Book Publishing Codes And Subject Headings For This Publication

BISAC EDI-Codes And Subject Headings For This Publication:
- MED026000 MEDICAL / Emergency Medicine
- MED024000 MEDICAL / Education & Training
- MED086000 MEDICAL / Test Preparation & Review
- MED058210 MEDICAL / Nurisng - Test Preparation & Review

Thema Codes And Subject Headings For This Publication:
- Medicine & Nursing
- MQF: First Aid & Paramedical Services
- MR: Medical study & revision guides & reference material
- 4CP: For vocational / professional education

Amazon Best Sellers Rank Subject Headings For This Publication:
- Books > Textbooks > Medicine & Health Sciences > Medicine > Clinical > Cardiology
- Books > Textbooks > Medicine & Health Sciences > Medicine > Clinical > Emergency Medicine
- Books > Medical Books > Medicine > Internal Medicine > Emergency
- Books > Medical Books > Medicine > Internal Medicine > Pathology > Diseases > Cardiovascular
- Books > ACLS

Bookstore Shelving / Sales Category:
- Medical > Test Preparation & Review

This Book Is Available From:
- Amazon
- Ingram

Dickson Keanaghan
Medical Publications

101 Medical Word-Search Puzzles
Have fun with the terms of art for 101
different medical subjects and specialties.

**QR Code for Dickson
Keanaghan's Website:**

The Zombie Notes Study Charts
ALL are current for 2017.
Each one is two pages long, and packed with info.
They can be downloaded for the kindle,
or purchased as a laminated card-stock.
Subjects: ACLS, BLS, PALS, ECG, Shock, Bradycardia,
ABG, and more related to these subjects.

Dickson Keanaghan
Medical Publications

ACLS Certification Exam Q&A With Explanations
Publication Date: November 2016
101 practice questions that cover every possible medical and
nursing scenario and topic on the ACLS certification exam.

PALS Certification Exam Q&A With Explanations
Publication Date: January 2017
101 practice questions that cover every possible medical and
nursing scenario and topic on the PALS certification exam.

BLS Certification Exam Q&A With Explanations
Publication Date: November 2016
101 practice questions that cover every possible medical and
nursing scenario and topic on the BLS certification exam.

Notes

CPSIA information can be obtained
at www.ICGtesting.com
Printed in the USA
LVOW06s1026170717

541634LV00018B/369/P